MEN-AT-ARMS SERIES

EDITOR: MARTIN WINDI

£5.50

The Malayan Campaign 1948-60

Text by JOHN SCURR

Colour plates by MIKE CHAPPELL

OSPREY PUBLISHING LONDON

Published in 1982 by
Osprey Publishing Ltd
Member company of the George Philip Group
12–14 Long Acre, London WC2E 9LP
© Copyright 1982 Osprey Publishing Ltd

Reprinted 1984, 1986, 1987

British Library Cataloguing in Publication Data
Scurr, John
    The Malayan Campaign 1948–60
    1. Malaya—History—Malayan Emergency
    I. Title
    959.5′1′p4   DS597

    ISBN 0-85045-476-X

Filmset in Great Britain
Printed in Hong Kong through Bookbuilders Ltd

Author's Note:
In preparing the text the author obtained information
from several published works and particularly from
regimental journals, too numerous to mention here.
Especially useful were two books: Gregory Blaxland's
The Regiments Depart (1971) and Anthony Short's *The
Communist Insurrection in Malaya, 1948–60* (1975).
Heartfelt thanks are extended to the Regimental
Secretaries of The Cameronians (Scottish Rifles),
Queen's Own Highlanders, Gordon Highlanders,
Light Infantry Office (Yorkshire), Royal Green
Jackets, Royal Hampshire Regiment, Royal West Kent
Regiment, Gloucestershire Regiment and 21 SAS
(Artists) Volunteers; and to the staffs of the Army
Historical Branch and Air Historical Branch, Ministry
of Defence, Imperial War Museum, RAF Museum and
Australian and New Zealand Defence Departments
(Army). Finally the author especially wishes to thank
Colonel Jon L. Sutro, OBE, MC, and Major James M.
Symes, MC (Retired), for their most generous co-
operation; and particularly Mike Chappell who, in
addition to his splendid paintings, contributed his
invaluable knowledge of uniforms and equipment.

The Emergency

In June 1948 Communist insurgent forces commenced a guerrilla war to end British rule in Malaya. This was, however, no ordinary rebellion against colonialism, but a conflict from which both the British administration and the people of Malaya were eventually to emerge triumphant.

Former British officers of the clandestine Force 136, which had liaised with the Malayan Communist Party and its guerrilla organisation—the Malayan People's Anti-Japanese Army—during the Second World War remembered the MCP's new Secretary-General, 26-year-old Chin Peng, as an intelligent and able person. Following the Moscow-sponsored Asian Youth Congress held in Calcutta in February 1948, Chin's Central Executive Committee approved a plan of political agitation and escalating terrorism in Malaya as part of a pattern of armed struggle throughout Asia.

Accordingly Lau Yew, former Chairman of the Central Military Committee of the MPAJA, began to call up his Chinese 'reservists' to form a Malayan People's Anti-British Army. Thousands of weapons which had been hidden in secret caches in the jungle in 1945 were unearthed and distributed. There was widespread murder and intimidation of Chinese, Malay and Indian workers in European-owned enterprises. Then, on 16 June 1948, three European managers were assassinated on two rubber estates near Sungei Siput in Perak. As a result the High Commissioner of Malaya, Sir Edward Gent, declared a State of Emergency in parts of Perak and Johore and, by the 18th of the month, this measure had been extended to the entire Federation of Malaya (population: 2,428,000 Malays, 1,885,000 Chinese, 531,000 Indians and 12,000 Europeans).

Operating from camps concealed in the fringes of the dense jungle which covered four-fifths of the country, the MPABA launched assaults upon village police stations, and continued their attacks on economic targets, particularly the rubber estates and tin mines. Barbed-wire fences were urgently erected around European bungalows and offices in the interior, while hastily-recruited Malay Special Constables were allocated to their defence. Although many British planters were killed on their isolated estates, the majority stubbornly refused to be driven out. Local people who refused to contribute food or subscriptions to the terrorists—particularly Chinese—were murdered or had their villages burned to the ground.

Following the death of Sir Edward Gent in an air crash near London on 4 July, Sir Henry

European lieutenant of Federation Special Police and Malay constables check the identity card of a Chinese vegetable grower, 1949. (BBC Hulton Picture Library)

The Forces Involved

Gurney, former Chief Secretary in Palestine, was installed as High Commissioner of Malaya on 6 October, and implemented some harsh measures to counter the desperate situation. People suspected of aiding the enemy were interned or deported to China in large numbers. Under Emergency Regulation 17D, made effective on 10 January 1949, inhabitants of entire villages could be detained at the High Commissioner's discretion. By October 1949 this regulation had been invoked 16 times and 6,343 people had been placed in detention camps; 10,300 Chinese had by then been deported.

The Communist Guerrilla Army

On 1 February 1949 the MPABA changed its title to Malayan Races Liberation Army. A Central Military Committee of the MCP, established in a jungle hideout in the Bentong area of Pahang, exercised command through North, Central and South Malaya Regional Bureaux, and then down through State, District and Branch Committees. When fully formed the MRLA had an overall strength of 5,000—increasing to a peak of 8,000 by 1951 of which 90 per cent were Chinese. The regiments were distributed in companies and platoons throughout the Federation as follows:

Northern Zone: 5th Regiment—Perak/West Kelantan; 8th—Kedah/Perlis; 12th Independent —North Perak/North Kelantan.

Central Zone: 1st Regiment—Selangor; 2nd—Negri Sembilan; 6th—West Pahang; 7th—South Trengganu; 10th—Central Pahang.

Southern Zone: 3rd Regiment—North Johore/Malacca; 4th—South Johore; 9th—Central Johore.

Each state also had independent companies or platoons, which roamed at will and were particularly aggressive. Supporting the MRLA at the outset were about 60,000 members of the underground Min Yuen (People's Movement), which operated in the villages and squatter areas providing food, funds and intelligence for the jungle regiments, as well as maintaining its own part-time armed units and 'killer squads'. Further support was rendered, either freely or under coercion, by up to half of the million-odd rural Chinese.

Both government and Security Forces referred to the MRLA's guerrillas as 'bandits' until early in 1952, when the more appropriate designation 'CTs' (Communist terrorists) was officially adopted.

The Security Forces

During the 12-year period from 16 June 1948 to 31 July 1960 the following British, Gurkha, Malayan and Commonwealth armed forces units participated in the conflict:

1st King's Dragoon Guards, 4th Queen's Own Hussars, 11th Hussars, 12th Royal Lancers 13th/18th Royal Hussars, 15th/19th King's Royal Hussars.

3rd Grenadier Guards, 2nd Coldstream Guards, 2nd Scots Guards, 1st Queen's Royal Regiment, 1st Royal Lincolnshire Regiment, 1st Devonshire Regiment, 1st Suffolk Regiment, 1st Somerset Light Infantry, 1st West Yorkshire Regiment, 1st East Yorkshire Regiment, 1st Green Howards, 1st Royal Scots Fusiliers, 1st Cheshire Regiment, 2nd Royal Welsh Fusiliers, 1st South Wales Borderers, 1st King's Own Scottish Borderers, 1st Cameronians, 1st Royal Innsikilling Fusiliers, 1st Worcestershire Regiment, 1st Royal Hampshire Regiment, 1st Sherwood Foresters, 1st Loyal Regiment, 1st/3rd East Anglian Regiment, 1st Queen's Own Royal West Kent Regiment, 1st King's Own Yorkshire Light Infantry, 1st Wiltshire Regiment, 1st Manchester Regiment, 1st Seaforth Highlanders, 1st

Guards patrol—believed to be 2nd Coldstreams—carry back a slain terrorist for identification by Special Branch. Note scrubbed 1937 pattern webbing equipment. Cameron Highlands, 1949. (Author's collection)

Gordon Highlanders, 1st Rifle Brigade, 22nd Special Air Service Regiment, Independent Parachute Squadron.

40, 42 and 45 Commandos, Royal Marines. 1st/2nd and 2nd/2nd King Edward VII's Own Gurkha Rifles, 1st/6th and 2nd/6th Queen Elizabeth's Own Gurkha Rifles, 1st/7th and 2nd/7th Duke of Edinburgh's Own Gurkha Rifles, 1st/10th and 2nd/10th Princess Mary's Own Gurkha Rifles. 1st, 2nd, 3rd, 4th, 5th, 6th and 7th Malay Regiment, 1st Singapore Infantry Regiment, 1st Federation Regiment (and Armoured Car Squadron), 1st, 2nd and 3rd King's African Rifles, 1st Northern Rhodesia Regiment, 1st Rhodesian African Rifles, 1st Fiji Infantry Regiment, 1st, 2nd and 3rd Royal Australian Regiment, 1st and 2nd New Zealand Regiment, Rhodesia Squadron (SAS), New Zealand squadron (SAS), Sarawak Rangers.

2nd, 25th, 26th and 48th Field Regiments Royal Artillery, 1st Singapore Regiment RA, 100th, 101st and 105th Field Batteries Royal Australian Artillery; 11th Independent Field Squadron Royal Engineers, 50th Gurkha Field Engineer Regiment RE, 51st Field Engineer Regiment RE, 74th Field Park Squadron RE, 75th Malayan Field Engineer Squadron, 410th Independent Plant Troop RE; 17th (Gurkha) Signal Regiment, 208th (Commonwealth) Signal Squadron, Malaya Command Signal Squadron; 55th Company Royal Army Service Corps (Air Despatch).

2nd Scots Guards set up 3in. mortars to bombard terrorist hideouts in Temerloh area of Pahang, 1949. (Imperial War Museum)

848 Naval Air Squadron; 28, 33, 45, 48, 52, 57, 60, 81, 84, 88, 97, 110, 155, 194, 205, 209, 267 and 656 Squadrons Royal Air Force; 91, 92, 93, 94, 95 and 96 Squadrons RAF Regiment (Malaya); 1, 2, 3, 38 and 77 Squadrons Royal Australian Air Force; 14, 41 and 75 Squadrons Royal New Zealand Air Force; and Penang, Singapore and Kuala Lumpur Squadrons Malayan Auxiliary Air Force.

Many ships of the Royal Navy, such as HMS *Amethyst*, *Comus*, *Defender*, *Hart*, *Newcastle* and *Newfoundland*, performed coastal patrol duties and gave fire support to land operations.

The Federation of Malaya Police

Colonel W. N. Gray, former Inspector-General of the Palestine Police, was appointed Police Com-missioner of Malaya in August 1948. Assisted by 500 freshly-arrived British police sergeants—the majority of whom were ex-Palestine Police and who were now granted officer status in the rank of lieutenant—Colonel Gray began to organise, train and equip his 10,000 predominantly Malay personnel, to create a police radio network, and to develop the new Special Branch. After six months 30,000 Special Constables and 15,000 part-time Home Guards, mostly Malays from the rural *kampongs* (villages), had been recruited.

Early in 1952 the regular police had reached a strength of 25,000, the SCs 39,000 and the HGs 100,000; and by 1953 the numbers of SCs and HGs had grown to more than 41,000 and nearly 250,000 respectively. Almost from the start the police had begun to take an active part in offensive operations with their own Jungle Squads. Two hundred such squads at the end of 1949 had increased to 500 a year later. During 1951–52 the Jungle Squads were re-organised, some into 22 Jungle Companies of the Federation Police Field

Force (each at an approximate strength of 180 men), while others were absorbed into Area Security Units in which SCs were now primarily committed to offensive action rather than static defence. By 1955 there were 556 of these Units, and 400 Mobile Operational Sections of HGs.

Scots Guards NCO lights a cigarette for an Iban tracker, 1950. The Iban's 'sword' was probably used by his head-hunting forebears in Sarawak. (BBC Hulton Picture Library)

Field Recognition Signs

On large-scale operations the risk of troops firing upon one another by mistake was minimised by the wearing of recognition signs on jungle hats. Some examples were as follows:

Operation Date	Area	Unit	Sign, where known
'Eagle' 27.1.53	Labis (N. Johore)	B Coy., 1st Cameronians / B Coy., 1st Fiji / B Sqn., 22 SAS	White bands for all units
'Cato' 16.3.53	Raub, Benta, Kuala Lipis (Pahang)	1st KAR	Yellow patch
		3rd KAR	Yellow circle
		6th Malay	Yellow band
		Sqn., 22 SAS	Yellow band
'Asp', 'Latimer South' 5.12.54	Tasek Bera, S. Palong, Fort Iskander, South Kongkoi (Pahang)	A Sqn., 22 SAS	None
		1st/7th GR	White square
		2nd/10th GR	White cross
		2nd RWF	Two white bars?
'Latimer North' 5.12.54	Tasek Bera, S. Palong, Fort Iskander, South Kongkoi (Pahang)	6th Malay	Yellow band?
		Police Field Force	Yellow spot
		Bahau Area Security Unit	White spot
		A Sqn., 11th Hussars	Regtl. berets
'Bee-hive' 27.11.55	Sy Ruia, Sy Kinta, Cameron Highlands (Perak)	D Sqn., 22 SAS	Blue band
		1st/6th GR	Orange 'VI'
		4th Malay	Yellow band
'Bee-hive' 11.12.55	Korbu Forest Reserve, Fort Brooke (Perak-Kelantan)	B Sqn., 22 SAS	Red band
		D Sqn., 22 SAS	Blue band
		1st/6th GR	Orange band
		4th Malay	Yellow band

Deployments

At the outbreak of the emergency in 1948 the GOC Malaya District, Maj. Gen. C. H. Boucher, had the following infantry units at his immediate disposal:

Northern Sub-District

1st Bn., King's Own Yorkshire Light Infantry; 2nd Bn., 2nd Gurkha Rifles; 1st Bn., 6th Gurkha Rifles; 1st and 2nd Bns., Malaya Regiment.

Central Sub-District

26th Field Regiment, Royal Artillery (converted to infantry rôle); 2nd Bn., 6th Gurkha Rifles; 1st and 2nd Bns., 7th Gurkha Rifles.

Johore Sub-District

1st Bn., Devonshire Regiment; 1st Bn., Seaforth Highlanders; 1st Bn., 2nd Gurkha Rifles; 1st Bn., 10th Gurkha Rifles.

Over the years the arrival, departure, and movements of numerous units involved frequent reorganisations. As a representative date one might quote September 1952, when the campaign was at its height and the GOC Malaya Command, Lt.Gen. Sir Hugh Stockwell, had the following infantry forces available:

Northern Malaya

1st Bn., 6th Gurkha Rifles; 1st and 3rd Bns., King's African Rifles; 1st to 6th Bns., inclusive, of the Malay Regiment; and the 1st Bn., Federation Regiment, under formation.

Central Malaya

18th British Infantry Brigade, comprising 1st Bn., Suffolk Regiment; 1st Bn., Worcestershire Regiment; 1st Bn., Royal West Kent Regiment; and, periodically, 1st Bn., Manchester Regiment, based on Penang.

Southern Malaya

26th, 48th, 63rd and 99th Gurkha Brigades, comprising: 1st and 2nd Bns., 2nd Gurkha Rifles; 2nd Bn., 6th Gurkha Rifles; 1st and 2nd Bns., 7th Gurkha Rifles; 1st and 2nd Bns., 10th Gurkha Rifles; 1st Bn., Green Howards; 1st Bn., Cameronians; 1st Bn., Gordon Highlanders; 22nd SAS Regiment; 1st Bn., Fiji Regiment.

The Jungle War

Lt. Gen. Sir Harold Briggs, Director of Operations (second on left) inspects a Federation Police Jungle Squad, 1950. (BBC Hulton Picture Library)

During 12 years of conflict there were 8,750 reported 'contacts' between units of the Security Forces and the Communist enemy. Only a very few can be related in this book—some chosen as particularly outstanding, and others merely as representative of innumerable other actions.

On 16 July 1948 the MPABA suffered a blow of incalculable gravity to its immediate plans when Police Superintendent Stafford and his squad of 14 Chinese and Malay detectives made a dawn raid on a hut near Kajang in Selangor (see Plate F2). The experienced and irreplaceable Chairman of the MCP's Military Committee, Lau Yew, was shot through the forehead as he raced, firing, from the hut. In the course of this initial exchange of fire, and subsequent skirmishes with some 30 to 50 bandits positioned on an adjacent hill, five other male terrorists and five females were all killed. The battle ended when a police charge up the hill finally put the enemy to flight.

Among the first British troops committed to offensive action were men of the 26th Field Regiment, Royal Artillery. Converted to an infantry rôle, the regiment proved its worth at the end of July when two batteries, operating with the Malayan Police at Batu Arang in Selangor, shared in the elimination of 27 terrorists.

At this same time an ex-Chindit officer, R.G.K. (later Sir Robert) Thompson of the government Planning Staff, and three former officers of Force 136 formed a special unit named Ferret Force, composed of volunteers from British, Gurkha and Malay battalions, the Malayan Police and Iban trackers from Sarawak. During its short existence of only a few months the 16 infantry sections of Ferret Force developed valuable operational techniques in the jungle. In September the Force also spearheaded a large-scale sweeping operation in which areas of the Johore jungle were strafed by Spitfires and painstakingly combed by the 1st Devons, 1st Seaforths, 1st Inniskillings and 1st/2nd and 1st/10th Gurkhas. Twenty-seven bandits were killed, 12 camps were located and destroyed, and large deposits of ammunition were discovered during this operation. These combined sweeps, which attempted to drive the enemy into waiting cordons of 'stops', were much favoured in this early period, but were later regarded as less effective than small patrols individually probing their battalions' own allotted areas.

Young soldiers, freshly arrived from Britain, could find themselves involved in sudden, deadly encounters. On 31 December 1948 two officers and 16 men of 4 Troop, A Squadron, 4th Hussars were patrolling in three vehicles along the Jalong road near Sungei Siput in Perak. About 70 bandits, whose armament included at least five Bren light machine guns, were dug in on high ground overlooking a bend in the uphill road, having lain for at least 24 hours in positions covering 300 yards of the road. The 4th Hussars were not supplied with armoured cars until the following year, and the patrol was therefore travelling in two GMC Personnel Carriers (with armoured protection at the sides but not over-

head) and a 15cwt. truck, the vehicles being spaced about 75 yards apart. When the bandits suddenly opened fire the 15cwt., in the centre of the convoy, was immobilised and most of the men on board killed. Newly commissioned 2nd. Lt. Sutro, in command of the rear GMC, then halted his vehicle and provided covering fire for the 15cwt.

Recalling the action, Col. Jon L. Sutro, OBE, MC, told the author:

'The first I saw of the opposition was when the barrel of a Thompson sub-machine gun appeared over the bank not more than 15 feet above me, followed by a very worried-looking Chinese, whom we promptly shot. There was another bandit position about 30 to 40 yards to the rear with a machine gun which inflicted several casualties until it was knocked out. The Troop Leader, Lt. Questier, was in the leading GMC. He showed enormous courage and leadership, and could have saved himself at the expense of those in the last GMC if he had chosen to do so. Instead he backed his vehicle some 100 yards or so until he reached the rear GMC.'

Police sergeant in bush hat instructing Malay Home Guards in the use of the No. 36 grenade, 1950. Dark-blue songkoks and HG armbands are the only uniform items worn. (Imperial War Museum)

The Hussars now leapt from their carriers and deployed on the road, determinedly returning the enemy's fire. Col. Sutro continued:

'Grenades were being rolled down a high bank and were exploding among us. Some were landing only a few feet away, but the blast generally went upwards and some of us survived by lying flat on the road. Michael Questier was killed a few yards from me by a grenade splinter between the eyes. One of the troop was killed by a base plug, and many others had wounds from splinters. I had a splinter which went into my left thigh and was removed from the other side of my leg in Ipoh Hospital the next day. I had another small splinter in my back which was left there and I felt a bullet nick the peak of my Service Dress hat.'

After holding the enemy at bay for about ten minutes, seven Hussars were dead and all but three of the remaining 11 were wounded. To avoid further casualties 2nd Lt. Sutro gave the order to re-board the two GMCs. With the dead and seriously wounded dragged on board, the two vehicles—one with flat tyres—were driven slowly forward under heavy fire to a point in a rubber plantation beyond which the road came to a dead-end by a river. Here the young officer organised his men in defence positions in some estate buildings and, after an unsuccessful attempt to contact his regiment by wireless, decided to go for help. Col. Sutro recalled:

'Trooper Goodier was unhurt, and volunteered to drive me back through the ambush position to bring reinforcements. He was a very brave man, as we had every reason to suppose that the position was still held by the terrorists.'

Nineteen-year-old 2nd Lt. Sutro was also a very brave man, and was justly awarded the Military Cross. Throughout the action his calm leadership had undoubtedly prevented greater loss of life. After being driven safely to Sungei Siput and telephoning his commanding officer, his only thought was to return to his men despite his wounds; however, a police officer restrained him. Six dead bandits found in the abandoned ambush positions were proof of 4 Troop's spirited defence.

A second award—the Distinguished Conduct Medal—was made to Tpr. Smith. Although twice wounded on the road, Smith crept around

Terrorist wounded and captured by military patrol, 1950. Although the Communists sometimes spared Malayan prisoners, no British soldiers who fell into their hands could hope to survive. (Imperial War Museum)

the flank of a terrorist position and, after opening fire with his rifle, was wounded once more. Proceeding further, he observed a party of 20 bandits marching up a track to reinforce the ambush, and shot the last man in the file. Bren gun fire from this party now wounded Tpr. Smith for a fourth time; but he managed to hide until nightfall, when he crawled back to the road. Reaching a hut by daybreak, he was given shelter by the Indian occupant, who then went to Sungei Siput to summon help.

A most successful action was fought on 11 January 1949 by a small patrol of the 1st Bn. King's Own Yorkshire Light Infantry. Sgt. Chadwick and just four other ranks of 11 Platoon, D Company were reconnoitring in a rubber estate near Karangan in Kedah when they spotted five bandits, 40 yards to their front, walking along beside a river. The bandits opened fire on the leading scout and took cover behind the river bank. Also diving into cover the patrol fired back and killed one of the bandits, whose body then floated downstream. The five KOYLI soldiers found it difficult to locate an adequate target due to the enemy's superior cover. Cautiously they crawled forward down the slope, drawing a hail of bullets at every movement. Then, on one of the

Men of D company, 1st KOYLI bury their dead at Batu Gajah civil cemetery, Perak, after a section had been ambushed in a defile near Ampang on 10 June 1950. Six soldiers were killed and one of the four wounded died a few days later. (Author's collection)

occasions when a terrorist leaned up to fire, they shot and killed him. For 15 minutes the exchange of fire continued. When a grenade was thrown at the patrol it fell short and rolled back down into the stream. As the soldiers edged still closer one of the bandits sensed that he was cornered and made a run for it. Jumping over a fence, he was brought down by another fatal volley from the patrol. There were now only two terrorists left—a man and a girl.

Sgt. Chadwick commented afterwards: 'The girl had been hit and would not give up. To enable her companion to reload his rifle she went on firing with her pistol. I left two men on the hill and took the rest down and crept up on them. We got to within a few yards while they were still firing at our chaps on the hill. We then opened up with all we had and both were killed.' Sgt. Chadwick was subsequently awarded the Military Medal.

During 1949 the MRLA largely withdrew to regroup and retrain, but towards the close of the year terrorist units, varying in size from 100 to 400 personnel, launched attacks upon rubber estates, tin mines, trains, road convoys, and police and government officials with renewed vigour.

For the Security Forces bandit-hunting could sometimes be costly. In the afternoon of 12 November 1949 a composite reconnaissance platoon of B Company, 1st Bn. Seaforth Highlanders located a temporary bandit camp in overgrown rubber west of the village of Chaah, in the Segamat district of Johore. On coming under fire the platoon drove some bandits from several lean-to *bashas* (shelters) to the north of the camp,

and was then engaged in a fierce exchange of fire with 150 to 200 terrorists positioned among other *bashas* to the south. Lt. Hoare, MC, and Lt. Anderson now advanced on the left flank to a point between two *bashas*, where Anderson could be seen behind a tree firing at the enemy. Up to this time only one man, Pte. Clarke, had been wounded, but L/Cpl. Mackay was then killed when the platoon came under heavy fire from many terrorist weapons, including at least three Bren guns.

After a counter-attack by the bandits had been vigorously repulsed the company commander, Maj. Campbell, ordered a withdrawal to a less exposed position 50 yards to the rear, but was then badly wounded. He gave a direct order to Lt. Brown to leave him and lead the platoon to its new position, which the lieutenant reluctantly obeyed. Almost immediately Maj. Campbell was again hit by a burst of fire and died. Under determined attack from the right flank of its new position the recce platoon was eventually reinforced from the company's temporary base to the rear. When the bandits withdrew, after one and a half hours of fighting, the Seaforths advanced into the camp and located six enemy bodies. They also found Lts. Hoare and Anderson, lying close to one another and both dead. Meanwhile a party of 20 bandits had approached B Company's base, but had fled after a sentry had killed one of them.

It was later established that the Seaforths' adversaries had been the ruthless 'Labis gang'. Early on 22 January 1950, in response to information received from Special Branch regarding a suspected camp of the same gang in the Segamat area, two platoons of B Company, 1st/2nd Gurkha Rifles, commanded by Maj. Richardson, were marching south through the rubber from the Ayer Panas road. Rfn. Bombahadur, near the centre of the extended formation, spotted an enemy sentry sprinting away towards a squatter's hut and shot at him. Several bandits then opened fire from in and around the hut. Without hesitation Bombahadur charged and, firing his rifle from the hip, killed at least four of the enemy. Maj. Richardson, ahead of most of the right-hand platoon, exchanged shots with a bandit, then turned to engage two others and shot both of them dead. The major then saw that the first bandit was now on his knees, chopping with a *parang* (long-bladed knife) at a Gurkha sprawled beneath him in the grass. Quickly firing again, Maj. Richardson killed the bandit, but it was too late to save the Gurkha soldier, who died later in hospital from severe slashes to the neck and skull.

In the meantime the left-hand platoon, led by CSM Bhimbahadur, swung round on the left flank and headed off the remainder of the bandits who were attempting to flee eastwards towards the sanctuary of the jungle beyond the Ayer Panas road. Forced to retreat westwards now through padi and swamps, the bandits were consequently caught in a deadly crossfire from both platoons. A later search revealed 22 enemy dead, though it was believed that there were more bodies in the swamp. Months later it was learned that the total of killed and fatally wounded had been 35 — the highest final score ever achieved.

For this action—which proved to be the most successful of the entire campaign—Maj. Richardson was awarded the Distinguished Service Order and CSM Bhimbahadur the Distinguished Conduct Medal.

If proof were needed that the Malayans were prepared to fight for their country, it was surely provided early in 1950. It was 4am on 23 February when 200 terrorists of the 4th Independent Company MRLA surrounded the police station at the isolated village of Bukit Kepong in Johore. Inside the station Sgt. Jamil hurriedly allocated his 20 Malay constables to defensive positions as the bandits opened fire from all sides. After an hour's heavy exchange of fire Sgt. Jamil was killed, but the constables continued to maintain a

Bandit camp, with accommodation for 100 personnel, found by 1st KOYLI in disused rubber estate bordering the jungle in North Malaya, 1950. (Imperial War Museum)

8 Platoon, C Company, 1st KOYLI halt for a rest in the Bongsu Forest Reserve, Kedah, late in 1950. Left to right: L/Cpl. Swalwell, Pte. Brodie, Pte. Busby and 'Steve', a Tamil Civil Liaison Officer—men with whom the author marched many a mile. (Imperial War Museum)

determined defence, repulsing several attacks against both the front and rear of the station and refusing all calls to surrender.

At daylight the terrorists mounted a massed assault, which this time smashed through into the rear of the compound. Soon the married quarters and the charge room were in flames and the Malay constables, still fighting, were shot down as they were driven out into the open. At one point during the assault Malay and Chinese Auxiliary Police from the village tried to aid the beleaguered station, but were driven back by the bandits with fatal casualties. It took 200 Communists five hours to overcome the 21 gallant defenders of Bukit Kepong. Thirteen Malay policemen, six auxiliaries, two wives and two children were killed. Several of these—some still alive—had been thrown into the blazing buildings. Three of the surviving constables were seriously wounded. The enemy had suffered at least seven dead and 15 wounded.

One month later, on 25 March, a platoon of D Company, 3rd Bn. Malay Regiment, stationed at Pulai in Kelantan, was ambushed in dense jungle on the south bank of the Semur River by a large force of bandits firing from shallow trenches prepared along the opposite bank. The platoon commander, 2nd Lt. Hassan, and several Malay soldiers were killed in the first fusillade, and others wounded. Cpl. Jamaluddin now took command, directing the fire of the remnants of the platoon,

who were pinned down along 150 yards of tracks. Calls to the platoon to surrender were answered with hails of bullets and several terrorists who tried to close in on the Malay soldiers were shot down.

Meanwhile Police Sergeant Wan Yaacob and 15 Special Constables, with whom the platoon had camped the previous night, hastened towards the sounds of battle, and split into two parties. Seven SCs came under fire and suffered casualties while trying to cross the river. The sergeant and the remainder, scouting round the flank of the terrorists' positions on the north bank, spotted an enemy Bren gunner and shot him dead, but then, on seeing that the platoon was being finally overwhelmed, wisely sought cover. Fifteen Malay soldiers lay dead along the track. Three more—gravely wounded—would die later. There were six others wounded, and only three men of the platoon remained unhurt. The severe casualties inflicted had, however, cost the enemy dear. Later examination of graves at the scene indicated that at least 29 bandits had been killed in the action.

On 21 March 1950 Lt.Gen. Sir Harold Briggs, a Burma veteran brought out of retirement, was appointed Director of Operations. Briggs formed a Federal War Council and State and District War Executive Committees in which representatives of the civil administration, the police and the military co-ordinated their policies. The principal intention of the 'Briggs Plan' was, commencing in the south, to provide security for the rural population while at the same time removing the main source of MRLA food supplies, funds and recruitment. This meant giving momentum to Sir Henry Gurney's scheme for transporting half a million Chinese squatters from their isolated clusters of shacks and vegetable patches, bordering the jungle fringes, to selected sites, enclosed by barbed-wire fences and guarded by SCs, initially known as Resettlement Areas and later as New Villages. Troops and police, descending on squatter areas before dawn, not unnaturally faced bitter resentment. Perhaps more than any other, however, this harsh measure proved crucial in defeating the terrorists.

A Soldier's Life

In Malaya (and in Korea) Britain's young National Servicemen proved that they could soldier with the best. After the inevitable 'green' period for new arrivals, hard experience ensured that neither National Servicemen nor Regulars remained 'virgin soldiers' for long.

The jungle in Malaya was even more formidable than the troops had experienced in Burma. In overgrown secondary jungle a patrol might barely cover a mile in four hours. Marching in file along a narrow track, with the overhead foliage completely shutting out the sun and the sky, soldiers had to push, and if necessary chop their way through dense thickets of saplings and attap-palms, festoons of creepers and clumps of bamboo. In primary jungle there would be giant, vine-covered tree-trunks with roots four feet high and ten yards long over which a patrol would have to clamber. Sometimes there would be fast-flowing rivers to wade across, or vast expanses of foul-smelling swamp.

The humid heat soaked soldiers in perspiration until they were visibly steaming, and summoned a thirst which experience taught them to quench only sparingly from their water-bottles. Leeches sought their vulnerable flesh and sucked out their blood: a man might find anything between five and 50 of the creatures clamped on to his body.

Iban tracker interprets signs found near a tin mine in Selangor to Sgt. Lister of 1st Suffolks, 1950. The sergeant is armed with an M2 carbine and the Iban with a Lee-Enfield No. 4 rifle. (Imperial War Museum)

Thomas Dewey, Governor of New York State, visits B Company, 1st Suffolks at Kajang, Selangor, accompanied by the regiment's CO, Lt.Col. P. A. Morcombe, OBE (on right), 30 July 1951. With totals of 181 terrorists killed and 15 captured against own losses of only 12 killed and 24 wounded during a normal three-year tour, the Suffolks by far outstripped every other unit as bandit-hunters. Two-thirds of the battalion's personnel were National Servicemen—i.e., conscripted 18-year-olds serving two years in the forces. (BBC Hulton Picture Library)

There were also vicious, biting red ants which showered upon them from the trees and jagged, trailing vines which ripped their skins and clothing. Worst of all was the mountainous nature of the terrain. As they climbed slope after slope, pulling themselves upwards by branches and roots and gulping the musty air of decaying vegetation into their winded lungs, soldiers became ever more aware of the leaden weight of their packs, weapons and ammunition and of the inevitable draining of their strength.

It is impossible to convey the feeling of utter exhaustion produced by a hard jungle march.

Sprawled out at the side of the track during a five-minute break, a man might feel so agonisingly spent that he would wonder if he would be able to stand up on his feet again. Yet, when the signal came to move on, he would somehow manage to continue placing one foot before the other, perhaps for hours after it had seemed that he had reached the limit of his endurance. Occasionally a soldier would collapse from heat exhaustion and might have to be evacuated.

When it was time to halt for the night the patrol would construct three-man shelters, known as *bashas*, by stretching waterproof poncho-capes over frameworks built from saplings. The night's sleep was invariably disturbed by swarms of whining mosquitoes, biting any exposed flesh and almost as easily through clothing. During the night each man endured a two-hour 'stag' (sentry duty), sitting alone in the dark behind a Bren gun at the edge of the bivouac area. Strange, dark shapes loomed around him and always moved if he looked at them too long, while a continuous cacophony of chirps, whistles, hoots and shrieks assailed him from all sides. The sudden crashing of a falling, rotted branch or the screaming of a monkey might make him start, while the rustling of something moving in the undergrowth would cause him to grip the cocking-handle of the Bren and wait anxiously. All the while the luminous hands of the guard-watch hardly seemed to move.

During the monsoon months marching soldiers were drenched at around 4pm every day by torrential rain, which could continue unabated for up to ten hours. Drainage furrows dug to divert rainwater were often inadequate to prevent *bashas* from being swamped. Consequently men might lie for a large part of the night trying to sleep in streams of muddy water pouring across their groundsheets. With so much fatigue and discomfort, plus the additional hazards of malaria, scrub-typhus, jaundice, dysentery, snake bites, scorpion stings, ulcerated jungle sores, tinea, ringworm, footrot and prickly heat, it might be supposed that soldiers had enough to contend with, but, of course, there was also the enemy.

Even in Communist-infested regions finding the enemy was far from easy (though men caught in sudden ambush might not agree). The largest terrorist camp encountered by the author was in the Bongsu Forest Reserve (Kedah) in April 1951. Sixty bandits, operating from this camp, had carried out some nasty ambushes in the Kulim district during the previous year; yet constant probing of the area had failed to locate the camp until a surrendered terrorist guided 8 Platoon, C Company, 1st KOYLI to it. On this occasion the platoon, commanded by 2nd Lt. Crisp, was unlucky. Two enemy look-outs on the approach track evaded the pursuit of the leading section, and when the platoon reached the camp it was found to have been hastily abandoned. The camp was concealed on a ridge and contained several large *bashas*, well constructed from bamboo and attap, incorporating living quarters with sleeping-platforms to accommodate 100, dining-hall, cookhouse and company office, all situated round a hard-earth combined parade ground and basketball pitch.

It had been four and a half months since 8 Platoon's previous contact, when a successful attack had been mounted against a smaller camp occupied by 30 bandits. The intervening 20 weeks of unrewarding 'jungle-bashing' were not the waste of time and energy which such periods often seemed, however. Documents taken from a captured terrorist revealed that the number of the company's patrols which were constantly searching the area (in conjunction with the local Police Jungle Squads) made it extremely difficult for units of the MRLA's 8th Regiment or their food suppliers to operate. Every patrol, in fact, harried the enemy one way or another.

Mike Chappell, the colour illustrator of this book, who served in Malaya with the 1st Royal Hampshire Regiment, told the author: 'All my operational experience was in the Bentong–Mentekab–Triang area of Pahang. The impression of spending thousands of hours in back-breaking toil for the sake of every contact is with me still. Like most of the other lads, I was usually off-guard and preoccupied with my burden, exhaus-

Men of 1st Cameronians displaying captured Communist flags and caps after the Iban tracker (crouching centre) led the patrol to a CT camp in Johore, 1951. (Imperial War Museum)

tion and thirst when a contact was made. What inevitably followed was brief and confusing. I never knew of one CT who stayed to fight.'

Sentry-posts and trip-wire alarms were placed fairly far out on the approaches to MRLA camps to give adequate warning of Security Forces patrols. It was standard procedure for the occupants of an attacked camp to flee by pre-arranged escape routes. At such times fast but accurate shooting with hard-hitting weapons was required. Mike recalls: 'At the BMH (British Military Hospital) Cameron Highlands, 22 SAS brought in a CT who was tied, struggling, to a stretcher. He had multiple wounds in his legs and body caused by 9mm rounds. These had penetrated such a short way that the bases of the rounds were visible. .303s in the stomach and neck had stopped him, and these were the only wounds that he had bandaged. Anyway, I never again carried a 9mm SMG of any sort after that.'

Sub-machine guns were, in fact, less effective than any other weapon, and would usually only bring an enemy down if he was hit in a vital organ. During the early years most kills were achieved with .30cal. American M1 and M2 carbines and .303 Bren light machine guns. Later these weapons were upstaged by 12-gauge Browning automatic and Remington slide-action shotguns, from which a multiple-pellet hit would invariably fell the target in a normal, close-quarter encounter.

Though some units undoubtedly became more expert at bandit-hunting than others, all tackled the task with great enthusiasm and courage. The author's favourite example of British Army spirit in the face of the enemy occurred when a small KOYLI patrol, pinned down in a disadvantageous position and outnumbered five to one, was surprised by a sudden halt in the terrorists' fire. Immediately a small but sturdy private yelled out: 'What's the matter, Johnny? Have you gone for a NAAFI-break?'

The Crucial Years

Although the principal task of the RAF Regiment (Malaya)— locally enlisted but with British officers and NCOs—was to defend airfields, two squadrons were normally employed in jungle operations under Army command.

At 1am on 21 March 1951, A Flight, 94 Rifle Squadron, commanded by Flying Officer Wright, proceeded from its base at Rawang in Selangor to mount a five-day ambush in the Ulau Simpan area. By dawn No. 1 Section was established in an ambush position while Nos. 2 and 3 Sections, under the command of Sgt. Taylor, set out to reconnoitre on the east side of Bukit Munchong. The 19-man patrol encamped near the top of this hill and the following morning, just before dawn, was awoken by the sentry's scream of 'Bandits!' as 40 to 50 terrorists launched attacks from the north, east and south, firing small arms and throwing grenades.

No. 2 Section Commander, Cpl. Ahmad, opened fire with his Sten gun, but was hit by a burst and severely wounded, while AFC Abdullah returned the enemy's fire with his Bren gun and rallied other Malay airmen around him. After being wounded in the arm, Sgt. Taylor was helped to cover behind a tree by LAC Mat, who now took over as Section Commander. AC2 Mahadi was then shot in the chest, but continued firing as he lay dying. Though his left arm was useless, Sgt. Taylor managed to fire his rifle and shot a crawling terrorist at 50 yards' range. The attacking groups of bandits were being directed by whistles and by a leader shouting orders from the top of the hill. LAC Mat shot this figure with his Sten gun, and scored at least one other hit before his ammunition was expended. Despite wounds in the knee and arm, AC1 Abdullah continued firing his Bren with only one arm until a third shot struck him in the chest and he collapsed over his gun.

After two hours four of the patrol lay dead and six were wounded (Cpl. Ahmad died the following day), and ammunition was running out. The bandits now closed in and forced the heavily outnumbered patrol to surrender. Sgt. Taylor feigned death and, fortunately, some of the Malay airmen managed to dissuade the terrorists from chopping off his head. The bandits then departed with the patrol's weapons and equipment. It was believed that at least four, and possibly eight of the enemy had been killed. LAC Mat and AC1 Abdullah were both subsequently awarded the Military Medal for their bravery.

A week leter, as Easter Monday dawned in the Slim area of Perak, a platoon of the Right Flank Company, 2nd Bn. Scots Guards charged into a terrorist camp, harrying the surprised bandits into the fire of a surrounding line of 'stops', which in turn drove the remnants back on to the bayonets of the attacking platoon. Ten bandits were killed in the process. Of the two who escaped, one was tracked and killed by the company a few days later and the other surrendered to the police. This great success was achieved during the Scots Guards' final week of operations in Malaya.

On 1 May 1951, men of 42 Commando, Royal Marines made a flying start to a month in which the unit was to kill 17 terrorists and capture five. Confronting a party of 25 CTs in a rubber estate west of Pusing in Perak, B Troop killed six of the enemy and wounded and captured two in a running fight. Later Capt. Mackay was fatally wounded in the head by enemy fire while leading a subsection of A Troop in a charge up a hill. One bandit was shot in return, but the troop subsequently suffered a second casualty when Lt. Johnson received a chest wound from which he was later to make a good recovery.

Another phase of the 'Briggs Plan' was initiated in June 1951. 'Operation Starvation' imposed strict food control checks on shopkeepers and villagers proceeding to the rubber estates and other work-places, in order to prevent food being smuggled out to the enemy. The 'Briggs Plan' had not yet stemmed the Communist offensive, however. On 6 October 1951 an independent platoon of 38 terrorists ambushed a Rolls-Royce limousine, escorted by a Police Land Rover on a bend of the road to Fraser's Hill, 40 miles north of Kuala Lumpur and, to their surprise, killed the High Commissioner of Malaya, Sir Henry Gurney.

Just over two weeks later, on the 22nd, another British reverse occurred when servere casualties were suffered by 11 Platoon, D Company, 1st Bn. Royal West Kent Regiment near Ulu Yam in Selangor. While returning from a routine three-day patrol the platoon was being carried in motor transport through the Ulu Caledonian rubber estate. An outburst of machine gun and rifle fire from small hills to the right of a bend in the estate road instantly killed the company commander, Capt. Deeds, and three soldiers in the leading 3-ton truck. The platoon commander, 2nd Lt. Gregson, was wounded twice in the first minutes, and the acting platoon sergeant, Cpl. Sulley,

Sgt. Beston and Sgt. Kibio of 1st (Nyasaland) King's African Rifles in September 1952. Their sleeves display the formation sign of HQ Malaya Command. (Imperial War Museum)

killed; but others from the first truck managed to take cover behind the left bank of the road. Meanwhile six men who had leapt out of a 15cwt. truck, 100 yards to the rear, were all killed by grenades slung down upon them from the

adjacent hill. Further back an armoured scout car was able to give little help, as enemy fire jammed the control gear of its mounted twin Bren guns.

Behind the left-hand bank of the estate road L/Cpl. Martin organised his four remaining men in firing positions. Pte. Pannell and the NCO both repulsed attacking groups of bandits with well-aimed hand-grenades before Martin was struck by a bullet in his shoulder. Not one of the

A trooper of a 14-man patrol of 22 SAS has been wounded in the head during a clash with terrorists in the Ulu Keneboi jungle, early in 1953. His comrades carry him in an improvised stretcher across a fast-flowing river to reach a clearing suitable for air evacuation. It takes one and a half hours to cover the 800 yeards' distance. (BBC Hulton Picture Library)

men was now unhurt, but all continued to return the enemy's fire, inspired by Pte. Pannell. Of this 37-year-old Regular soldier, one of the other ambushed men, Pte. New, declared: 'Although wounded in four places, he crept along the battle line in a ditch, shouting to us to fight back and directing our fire. When the bandits charged he killed one with a Sten-gun burst.'

Suddenly the dwindling group was reinforced behind the bank by a planter and four policemen, who jumped from a car which had raced up the estate road. Their combined firing now drove the CTs into retreat towards the nearby jungle, leaving six dead behind and taking several wounded with them. After 90 minutes of battle one West Kents

The SAS patrol has cleared a Landing Zone with machetes and explosives: note tree trunks piled on left. An RAF Dragonfly Mk II (S-51) hovers above the LZ with a basket-stretcher visible on the left side ready to be lowered. The casualty reached Kinrara Military Hospital eleven hours after he was wounded. (BBC Hulton Picture Library)

Captured Chinese terrorist, in KD uniform, puttees and red-starred cap, poses with his double-barrelled shotgun: 1953. (BBC Hulton Picture Library)

officer, ten other ranks and three Iban trackers lay dead, while one officer, 11 ORs and one CLO (Civil Liaison Officer) had been wounded. One of the five seriously wounded would die later. For their outstanding bravery L/Cpl. Martin was awarded the Military Medal and Pte. Pannell the Distinguished Conduct Medal.

In 1951 alone there were 6,082 recorded terrorist incidents and 1,911 contacts, in which 533 civilians, 354 policemen and 124 soldiers were killed. 1,078 bandits were also killed, 121 captured and 201 surrendered, thereby increasing the total of Communists eliminated in the previous year by a half. In December Gen. Briggs retired with rapidly failing health and died a few months later.

In February 1952, a figure arrived on the scene who was radically to transform the whole situation. Lt.Gen. Sir Gerald Templer, who had been both a divisional and a corps commander during the Second World War, was appointed to fulfil the combined functions of High Commissioner and Director of Operations. Templer reinvigorated the flagging 'Briggs Plan', and urged closer liaison between the different elements of the State and District War Executive Committees. At the same time he raised civilian morale by underlining the British government's stated intention that Malaya would be granted independence, with its own democratically-elected government, as soon as the security situation permitted.

Templer travelled extensively around Malaya in his armoured car, and intervened personally to solve many problems. Though tough, and even ruthless, with both friend and foe in his determination to wipe out Communist terrorism, he was unquestionably dedicated to the people of Malaya. Chinese resettled in the New Villages were encouraged to take responsibility for their own affairs and, in May 1952, elected representatives to village councils. In September Templer granted full citizenship to all aliens born in Malaya, which he hoped would contribute towards forging a united Malayan nation.

The MRLA, in the meantime, was in a process of reorganisation. A meeting of the MCP's Central Executive Committee in Pahang in October 1951 had resolved to attempt to cut their increasing casualty rate by reducing the size of their fighting units from companies of 100 or more to platoons of 20 or 30, which the Security Forces would find more difficult to locate and destroy. It was well into 1952, however, before all MRLA units had received and adapted to this instruction. Another meeting of the Executive Committee, in April 1952, prudently decided to transfer Chin Peng's headquarters to Betong, across the border in southern Thailand.

Welcome reinforcements to the Security Forces, early in 1952, were the 1st Bn. Fiji Infantry Regiment and 1st (Nyasaland) and 3rd (Kenya) Bns. King's African Rifles. Tremendously fit and agile, with many New Zealand officers, the

Fijians operated in Johore. They favoured patrols of about five men; if an enemy camp was located one Fijian would kill the sentry while the other four charged the camp, irrespective of the possible size of the opposition. At other times, on operations of platoon or company strength, patrols of only two men each would probe in different directions from a central jungle base. On finding a camp one man would remain to keep watch while the other returned to the base to bring an assault party.

Once they gained experience the KARs soon adapted their African tracking techniques to this new terrain. In July 1952 the 3rd (Kenya) Bn. was contributing to two concurrent operations in Pahang: two companies supported the 1st/10th Gurkha Rifles in the Kuantan coastal region, and the remainder co-operated with the 1st (Nyasaland) KARs, 4th Malay Regiment and No. 12 Federal Jungle Company (Malayan Police) in the Triang area. In these operations the 3rd (Kenya) killed a total of 11 CTs, four of whom met their end when askaris, uttering tribal war cries, chased them through the jungle and struck them all down with *pangas* (large African knives). By the end of their 18-month tour the 3rd (Kenya) had killed more than 60 terrorists.

Meanwhile British troops continued to hunt the enemy with increased success. In the early hours of 12 June 1952, guided by an SEP (Surrendered Enemy Personnel), Capt. Bagnall and ten men of the Machine Gun Platoon, 1st Bn. Green Howards, crept into position on two sides of an MRLA main camp in the Tampin Forest Reserve, Negri Sembilan. Just before dawn a CT suddenly walked out of the camp to undertake his duty at the daytime sentry-post. Positioned behind a tree directly in the terrorist's path, Capt. Bagnall shot him dead. The entire patrol then opened fire in poor light upon CTs fleeing from the *bashas*, killing three inside the camp and three outside. Capt. Bagnall was awarded a bar to his Military Cross for this action.

The 1st Bn. Suffolk Regiment had waged a constant war in South Selangor against the MRLA's 4th Independent Company, known as the 'Kajang gang', for three years. Then, one happy day in July 1952, Special Branch relayed information that the gang's bearded leader Lliew Kon Kim and No. 3 Platoon of his company

Bren gunner of 1st Royal West Kents advances through the Selangor jungle, 1953. Note ripped, sweat-soaked shirt and mud-stained equipment. (BBC Hulton Picture Library)

were to be found in a camp in the Kuala Langat south swamp.

The Suffolks, aided by two companies of the Royal West Kents, waded for three days through the south swamp, ten miles by eight in area, in search of the camp. After numerous brief contacts fresh information, obtained from a captured

Royal West Kents rifleman on patrol in 1953, being drenched by the daily downpour, which was usually accompanied by a thunderstorm. (BBC Hulton Picture Library)

Min Yuen agent, revealed that Lliew could be found in an area to the north of the New Brighton estate. Consequently B Company of the Suffolks, commanded by Maj. Dewar, began to search through the indicated area in nine patrols moving parallel and guided by the informer. This man soon appeared hopelessly lost; however, the company discovered fresh CT tracks in the area and, on 6 July, was again advancing in nine parallel patrols through the swamp when, at 2pm, 2nd Lt. Hands and his two scouts, Ptes. Baker and Wynant (all three were National Servicemen), spotted a terrorist disappearing into the undergrowth ahead. They immediately opened fire and, running along a log, came suddenly into a small camp on an island and saw three CTs scurrying from one of the *bashas*. 2nd Lt. Hands fired a burst from his MI carbine, killing one of the enemy. Dashing in pursuit of the others as fast as the murky, thigh-deep swamp would permit, he followed the sounds of splashing and put another fatal burst of fire into a second CT, a woman armed with a shotgun. Hurrying forward for another 150 yards the young officer sighted the third CT, fired once more and, on approaching the fallen figure, found that this time he had killed none other than the bearded Lliew Kon Kim. For his excellent work 2nd Lt. Hands was awarded the Military Cross.

By this time small patrols, moving silently, learning to track and to listen for sounds of the enemy, were earning their reward. During 1952, 1,155 terrorists were killed, and this year proved to be the turning-point in the campaign. With the resettlement of the Chinese squatters largely completed and the security situation improved Gen. Templer felt able, in March 1953, to abolish the much-hated Emergency Regulation 17D which had permitted mass detentions. By then 29,828 people had been detained since June 1948. Concurrently, food restriction policies were being more strictly and successfully implemented, particularly through curfews and search operations.

It had been known for some time that food was being supplied to the enemy from a New Village called Buloh Kasap, eight miles from Segamat in Johore. All efforts to locate the supply route had drawn a blank until finally a Special Branch agent, planted in the village, arranged to deliver a large stock of food to a terrorist leader called Wong Piew.

After dark on the night of 14 April 1953, ambush parties of the 1st Bn. Cameronians moved silently into position, both at the south-west of the village's perimeter-fence and at likely escape routes back to the jungle. As 2nd Lt. Weir was leading one of three small groups from C Company to its intended position near the perimeter, the party was suddenly fired on in the darkness from a range of about ten yards. L/Cpl. Tweedie was wounded in the ensuing exchange of fire and at least two hits were claimed by the Cameronians before their attackers finally fled. Meanwhile Maj. Kettles and Lt. Baynes, with an ambush party from the Machine Gun Platoon, had positioned themselves in the rubber by the main Buloh Kasap estate road. After two hours a flashing light to the front of their position indicated someone with a torch moving through the trees. Sounds of approaching men drew closer until a CT suddenly appeared just four yards in front of the Battalion Signals Officer, Lt. Campbell. A long burst from the officer's Bren gun brought the CT down, and the remainder of the ambush party immediately opened fire. The floating lights of Verey pistol cartridges revealed a terrorist collapsing in a swamp to the right and another nearby, apparently badly wounded. At an adjacent position, five minutes later, Sgt. Hannah of the Mortar Platoon fired a few bursts at a figure running along a footpath through the swamp.

That night only the body of the CT shot by Lt. Campbell was found; but the following morning, during a search by the Anti-tank Platoon along the edge of the swamp, Rfn. Frew and Fisher surprised and killed a wounded but still armed terrorist amongst the thick rushes. Meanwhile a body had been dragged from the swamp by the estate road, and blood trails were found on the footpath where Sgt. Hannah had fired. The score was now three CTs killed, one of whom was identified as the leader, Wong Piew, and it was believed that there must be another body somewhere in the swamp.

Early in 1953 ten helicopters of 848 Naval Air Squadron were employed in experimental operations, lifting troops into the jungle. Between March and June men of the 1st and 3rd KARs,

1: Australian Captain, 1953
2: CSM, 1st Royal Hampshires, 1954
3: Gen. Sir Gerald Templer, 1952
4: Sergeant, Glider Pilot Regt., 1950s
5: Gurkha Rifleman, 1950s

99th Gurkha Bde.

2nd Guards Bde.

A

1: Constable, Federation of Malaya Police, 1949-50
2: Woman Police Constable, early 1950s
3: Police Commissioner A. E. Young, 1952
4: Police Aboriginal Guard, 1955

Cap-badge, all three figures wearing headgear

1: Junior NCO, 1st Royal Hampshires, 1954
2: Private, 1st Devonshires, 1948
3: Guardsman, 2nd Scots Guards, 1949

C

1: Infantry signaller, 1951
2: Infantry leading scout, early 1950s
3: Iban tracker, early 1950s

D

1: Company commander, MRLA, early 1950s
2: Min Yuen member, 1950s
3: Soldier, 32nd Independent Ptn., MRLA, 1954

E

1: Police Sergeant, Jungle Squad, 1951
2: Police Superintendent Stafford, 1948
3, 4: Aborigines, mid-1950s
5: Sergeant, Gurkha Rifles, 1948

F

1: Trooper, 22nd SAS Regt., 1954
2: RM Commando, 1951
3: Corporal, 1st KOYLI, 1950
4: Captain, 1st Cameronians, 1952
5: Squadron-Leader, 81 Sqn. RAF, 1959

1: Captain, 2nd KAR, 1953
2: Private, 1st Gordon Highlanders, 1952
3: Lieutenant, 848 Naval Air Sqn., 1953
4: Trooper, 11th Hussar, 1953
5: Iban tracker, 1952
6: Private, Malay Regt., 1955

HQ Malaya Command

Air Despatch Organisation

6th Malays, 1st East Yorks, 2nd/6th and 2nd/10th Gurkhas and 1st Manchesters were all involved in operations in Kelantan, Johore and Pahang in which helicopters of this squadron flew the troops into located areas where it was hoped to net MCP Committee Members and other MRLA commanders. These operations were only partially successful. The advantage of speed was countered by the difficulty of finding suitable clearings in the jungle for descent.

On 3 September 1953 the first 'White Area', considered sufficiently free from terrorist activity for all Emergency restrictions to be lifted, was declared in a coastal region of 221 square miles in Malacca, to be followed during the next few months by areas of Trengganu, Perlis, Kedah and Negri Sembilan. By December there were only 2,225 people still held in detention camps. During 1953 the MRLA lost 959 killed, 73 captured and 372 surrendered. Many more died in the jungle from untreated wounds, malnutrition, malaria, beri-beri, dysentery, and execution for 'deviation'. The overall strength now stood at around 6,000, concentrated mainly in Pahang, Perak, Johore and Negri Sembilan.

Gen. Templer ended his period of office on 30 May 1954 and, the following month, left Malaya knowing that its people now had the confidence both to defeat Communist insurgency and, very shortly, to govern themselves. Though not yet prepared to admit it, Chin Peng and his 'liberation army' had failed.

The Deep Jungle

At the close of 1950, during a drive by 45 Commando, RM against hostile aborigines in a region between Tapah and the Cameron Highlands in Perak, Capt. Wild and Marine Blythe of S Troop had the rare experience of being wounded by poisoned darts without fatal consequences. In fact the nomadic, aboriginal tribes that inhabited Malaya's central mountain range were concerned only with survival, and were therefore prepared to support whichever side appeared to be on the ascendant in their region.

The need for a special deep jungle unit prompted Maj. J. M. Calvert, Burma veteran and former commander of the Special Air Service Brigade in Europe during the Second World War, to instigate recruitment towards the end of 1950 for the Malayan Scouts. One hundred volunteers, including former members of the SAS, Force 136 and Ferret Force, were formed into A Squadron, which undertook its first operations in small teams in the jungle around Ipoh in Perak. In January 1951 A Sqn., Malayan Scouts, was reinforced by B Sqn., composed of reservists from the Territorial unit 21 SAS. Volunteers from Rhodesia soon arrived to constitute C Sqn., while a fourth (D Sqn.) was raised towards the end of the year. From this foundation a new regiment was born in May 1952—22nd Special Air Service.

The regiment specialised in the hazardous technique of parachuting into the tree-tops and then lowering themselves to the ground, a technique first employed operationally, in February 1952, in the Belum Valley near the Thai border. During 1952, as Communist casualties mounted and food sources were increasingly denied them, many MRLA platoons were withdrawn into the deep jungle, where they relied on the aborigines to supply them with food and shelter and to act as a screen against the Security Forces. The MCP's aim was to establish safe deep jungle bases, with their own cultivation plots, from which a fresh offensive could eventually be launched. To counter this increasing domination of the 50,000 jungle-dwellers, SAS troops landed by helicopter or parachute in remote regions to locate the aborigines and regroup them in protected areas and, where possible, eliminate the local CTs. These operations were normally of 13 weeks' duration, during which the troops were resupplied by airdrop.

On 10 April 1953 the Malayan government announced that, with the approval of the Sarawak administration, Iban volunteers would be formed into a fighting unit to be called the Sarawak Rangers. Iban descendants of Sarawak head-hunting tribes had been serving six-month engagements with the Civil Liaison Corps since August 1948, allocated as trackers to British units. The original 47 had grown to an average strength of 200. Subsequently trained by 22 SAS, the Sarawak Rangers made an enthusiastic contribution to deep jungle operations.

NCO of Royal West Kents checks that his patrol's weapons are unloaded after return to the company base, in 1953. Second man from left has an Australian Owen gun, while the NCO carries an American M2 carbine. Note individual styles of jungle hats. (BBC Hulton Picture Library)

Especially active in the task of persuading the jungle people to support the government was the Department of Aborigines. By the end of 1953 more than 200 Malay Field Assistants and Aborigine Field Staff were providing medical clinics, schools and trading posts. These facilities were established in seven jungle forts, garrisoned by platoons of the Police Field Force and regularly supplied by air. Eventually, by 1955, there would be ten forts strategically placed in Perak, Kelantan and Pahang.

Between July and November 1954 the largest operation in the campaign so far, Operation 'Termite', was mounted in Perak, in the deep jungle east of Ipoh. RAF Lincolns carried out heavy bombing of suspected hideouts, after which 177 men of three squadrons of 22 SAS parachuted into the clearings blasted by the bombs. The 1st West Yorks, 1st Royal Scots Fusiliers, 1st/6th Gurkhas, 5th Malays and other elements then closed in, some transported by helicopter. Though all the time and trouble only eliminated 15 terrorists, many camps and supply dumps were located. On the other hand, the aborigines in the area were terrified by the bombing and fled. While it could be said that this removed them from

previous Communist domination, it would be a long and difficult task to locate these aborigines and bring them into the government fold.

Late in 1955 22 SAS was reinforced by the arrival from Britain of the Parachute Regiment Squadron and, in December, the departed Rhodesian Squadron was replaced by another from New Zealand. Commanded by Maj. Rennie and comprising Squadron HQ and four Troops, the New Zealand Squadron had 133 carefully selected personnel, a third of whom were Maoris. Commencing in April 1956, the squadron undertook two 13-week operations on the Perak-Kelantan border during which it smashed a Communist Asal (aborigine) organisation. The first of eight CTs killed was the gang's notorious leader, Ah Ming, who had dominated the aborigines of the Fort Brooke area since 1948. Ah Ming and another terrorist, Kwun Pun, were cut down by automatic fire at first light on 27 April after an aborigine called Alok had guided 3 Troop, commanded by Lt. Burrows, for three days along a trail which was quite indiscernible to the New Zealanders. The following month 2 Troop, led by Lt. Glandell, located and cautiously approached a small CT camp. Opening fire with four Bren guns at ten yards range, the troop was enabled to kill four of the camp's five occupants.

Aborigines had been encouraged to contribute to offensive operations: first in the AAPs (Aboriginal Auxiliary Police), who acted mainly as guides and porters for the Police Field Force, then in 19 sections of the PAGs (Police Aboriginal Guards), who were permitted to carry out reconnaissance work. However, R. O. D. Noone, Protector of Aborigines, had felt for some time that the aborigines' operational potential was not being fully utilised, as did Lt.Col. G. H. Lea, commanding officer of 22 SAS. Consequently four sections of ten aborigines each were formed by the Department of Aborigines at the end of 1956, and trained by 22 SAS. Within a year the Senoi Pra'ak (Fighting People) had three squadrons, each with 12 five-man sections which could operate independently in the search for small terrorist bands and remaining hostile aborigine groups.

Meanwhile 22 SAS had continued to wean the jungle-dwellers away from the Communists and to hunt down recalcitrant hostiles and their CT masters. During 14 weeks of operations commencing on 2 May 1956, B Sqn. succeeded in converting 180 aborigines and locating 350 acres of the enemy's crops in the extreme north of the Perak-Kelantan border area, killing two terrorists and wounding four in the process. In this same region, at the end of August, a small patrol of 17 Troop, D Sqn., consisting of Sgt. Turnbull (famed for his speed and accuracy with his automatic shotgun) and three troopers, tracked four CTs for five days. Eventually hearing voices in a clump of bamboo, Sgt. Turnbull reconnoitred and spotted the terrorists' sentry. The patrol now waited until the sentry withdrew into a *basha* during a rainstorm, then crept up on the *basha* and killed all four terrorists in a short, sharp engagement. Sgt. Turnbull was subsequently awarded the Military Medal.

In February 1958 37 men from D Sqn., commanded by Maj. Thompson, parachuted into the 180-square-mile Telok Anson swamp in Selangor, where they tracked two groups of CTs for 14 weeks and finally forced them to surrender. After a year of little reward in 1958 the Senoi Pra'ak achieved numbers of kills and captures in 1959 which, though small, were larger than those gained by any other military or police unit during that year.

From January 1960 the 2nd Bn. New Zealand Regiment was deployed on operations along the Thai border, based in the jungle forts of Upper Perak. During seven months in that wild region the battalion captured four terrorists.

Gen. Sir Gerald Templer, High Commissioner of Malaya, jokes with an ex-terrorist now serving with the Special Operations Volunteer Force, at the Federation Police Jungle Company Training Centre at Sungei Buloh, near Kuala Lumpur, on 12 June 1953. One hundred and eighty former terrorists, in 12 platoons, undertook operations against their erstwhile comrades. (Associated Press)

The Final Push

Concurrent with the gradual pacification of the deep jungle of the central mountain range, operations were continuing elsewhere in Malaya. From June 1954 until June 1955 Operation 'Apollo' combed 3,464 square miles of territory in the Kuala Lipis region of Pahang and netted 69 terrorists, 18 of whom were killed by the 2nd/7th Gurkha Rifles. In Operation 'Nassau', commenced on 21 December 1954, the 1st Royal Hampshires spent eight months wading knee—and sometimes waist—deep through the 100 square miles of the south swamp in the Kuala Langat district of South Selangor. Seeking an independent platoon of 37 CTs, the Hampshires were finally rewarded by 'bagging' 19 of the enemy, while the elimination of a further 16 was shared by the 1st Fiji and 7th Malays. Suspected CT locations were bombarded throughout this operation by artillery, Lincoln bombers and coastal patrolling ships of the Royal Navy.

A total of 723 terrorists had been killed during 1954; and by 1955 the depleted 3,000-strong MRLA was becoming harder to find, the number of contacts being just over half that of the previous year. However, CTs continued to surrender—211 in 1954 and 249 in 1955. These surrenders were often the result of food denial operations aimed at blocking supply lines to terrorists in a specific area over a period of several months. By April 1955 areas of Pahang and Trengganu had been declared 'White'; and at the end of July Malaya held its first general election. As a result Tunku Abdul Rahman, leader of the UMNO (United Malay National Organisation), headed a Triple Alliance government—a coalition of his own party, the MCA (Malayan Chinese Association) and the MIC (Malayan Indian Congress), who had all previously been mutually distrustful of one another. This new co-operation boded well for the future.

Special Branch information obtained from an SEP in Selangor led to a very successful action in December 1955. The deserter had indicated that a course of political instruction for high-ranking CTs was being held in a camp within the jungle fringe, near the village of Ulu Langat. Con-

Patrol of the Federation Police Field Force crosses the Temengor River, Upper Perak, 1954. The leading scout is armed with a Sten SMG and the second with a Browning automatic shotgun. (Imperial War Museum)

sequently, on the night of 10 December, a composite company of 4 and 6 Platoons, B Company and 10 Platoon, D Company, 1st Bn. Royal Hampshire Regiment, commanded by Maj. Symes (OCB Company), set out to attack the camp.

Guided by Police Inspector Alias and the SEP, nicknamed 'George', the company had no success in locating the objective throughout the 11th. After the force appeared to have strayed too far to the west, a fresh bearing was taken and a reconnaissance verified a route which brought the Hampshires across the Sub River; but George was unable to find the vital track until nightfall. At 7 am on the following day Maj. Symes led the company northwards. George now recognised the area and, by 9am, had cautiously guided Maj. Symes and a reconnaissance group to within sight of the camp, which was situated on a steep spur flanked by two streams, beyond which were two ridges, all running roughly from north to south.

With the sounds of their movements obliterated at first by heavy rain, the Hampshires took all of four hours to quietly surround the camp. The assault party, composed of Company HQ and half of 10 Platoon, was positioned along a track on a slope to the north-west of the camp, while the other half of 10 Platoon was deployed to the west as part of the encircling cordon, completed by 6 Platoon to the south-west and south and 4 Platoon to the east and north-east. At 1.20pm Maj. Symes gave the signal to advance. Three assault groups, each of four or five men, commanded by Maj. Symes, Sgt. Hogan and Cpl. Smith, were to advance directly on the camp while Capt. Chandler led a fourth group to intercept an expected sentry and then move in from the north.

Maj. James M. Symes, MC (now retired), told the author: 'About ten yards down the slope I yelled: "Charge!" and fired my M1 carbine at a *basha* 20 yards away almost on the crest of the knoll. The rest of the party opened fire; then we slid down the slope, crossed the stream and started to clamber up towards the camp through saplings and undergrowth. It was a sharp incline and very muddy from the recent rain. A single shotgun blast directed at us passed over harmlessly. Then we were in the camp—all three groups—but the terrorists had bolted, leaving the place in a shambles.'

Capt. Chandler's group arrived minutes later. Of the sentries supposed to be posted to the north and west there had been no sign. Fleeing both south and east, the CTs tried desperately to escape. A group of eight ran southwards straight into fire from 6 Platoon, which killed at least three and drove the remainder eastwards across the stream, only to be shot down by the waiting men of 4 Platoon.

Maj. Symes recalled: 'George had known exactly which escape routes the terrorists would take and where we should place the "stops". The two platoons exercised good fire discipline, and I would say the number of rounds expended was extremely low. The boys waited till they saw the whites of their eyes, and let them have it with Brens, shotguns and FN rifles.' (In 1955 the Royal Hampshires had been selected for trials of the Belgian FN self-loading Rifle.)

There was sporadic firing for 20 minutes. When the cordon parties were called in to search the area, it was found that 4 Platoon had killed six CTs and 6 Platoon five. A wounded female terrorist, lying in a thicket, was taken prisoner.

Maj. Symes commented: 'She was a real bitch and very hostile, even when one of the young subalterns tried to help her by applying a dressing to the wound in her thigh. Still, I suppose it was understandable under the circumstances.'

The only other woman in the camp had been killed. Also among the dead were the Selangor State Committee Secretary, Chan Lo, and a District Committee Member, Wahab. On 22 December the Branch Committee Secretary, Sarlip, was captured by a Hampshires patrol. He

Maj. James M. Symes, MC, 1st Royal Hampshire Regiment, who led the attack on a CT camp at Ulu Langat on 12 December 1955 (see text). His left sleeve displays the formation sign of the Wessex Brigade Group. (Royal Hampshire Regiment)

New Zealand SAS on patrol along the Perak/Kelantan border in 1956. Note Bergen rucksacks. The first trooper carries a Browning shotgun, the second an MI carbine. (New Zealand Defence Department)

the darkness to select ambush positions, and were suddenly aware of something on the ground just in front. Instinctively they opened fire in the pitch blackness, and several forms darted away. As the day dawned it was discovered that seven CTs had been sleeping in the open under mosquito-nets and that at least two had been hit. On the ground lay the dead body of Yeong Kwo, Vice-Secretary General of the MCP (second-in-command to Chin Peng). A blood trail showed that a seriously wounded man had escaped.

During 375,849 sorties by aircraft of the RAF, RN and Australian and New Zealand squadrons the valuable contributions of air supply and casualty evacuation were supplemented by air-strikes in which 33,000 tons of bombs and 100,000 rockets were released against unseen and often non-existent targets in the jungle. On 21 February 1956 Political Commissar Goh Peng Tuan and 13 members of the 7th Independent Platoon, MRLA were killed when a squadron of RAAF Lincolns obliterated a camp near Kluang in Johore by dropping 90,000lbs. of bombs in a rectangle of 700 × 400 yards, which was afterwards strafed by two squadrons of RAF Canberra jets. Similarly, RAAF Lincoln bombers killed the leader of the 3rd Independent Platoon, Tan Fuk Leong, and four others near Seremban in Negri Sembilan on 13 May 1957. In both instances, however, the targets were precisely pinpointed through Special Branch information and, in the case of the former, also by expert reconnaissance by a patrol of the 1st South Wales Borderers.

Thirty thousand square miles out of 50,850 had become 'White Areas' by July 1957, and on 31 August Malaya achieved full independence from Britain, remaining within the Commonwealth. The 1st New Zealand Regiment arrived in December and commenced operations in Perak with the 28th Commonwealth Brigade in March 1958. In one year and nine months of constant patrolling the 1st New Zealand eliminated 28 CTs for the loss of three of its own men and an attached Sarawak Ranger, an excellent record for that late period, which was unsurpassed by any other unit in the Brigade.

had been wounded during the attack and disclosed that he had, in fact, been the sole survivor. With 11 CTs killed and one captured, this classic action had given the Royal Hampshires the highest score of any company engagement since early 1950, and the highest total of terrorists eliminated in one encounter recorded by any British battalion.

The 28th Commonwealth Brigade, which had gained fame in the Korean War, was revived in October 1955 when the 2nd Royal Australian Regiment arrived in Malaya, accompanied by a battery of field artillery. Also encompassing the 1st Royal Scots Fusiliers and a New Zealand engineer squadron, the brigade undertook operations in Perak during 1956. Contacts with the enemy throughout Malaya were considerably reduced that year, and troops were increasingly employed on food control and search operations.

Freshly arrived from Kenya the 1st Bn., The Rifle Brigade made a spectacular first kill on 26 August 1956, near Semenyih in South Selangor. Following a Special Branch tip-off, 7 Platoon, B Company was guided by a Police Inspector through a rubber estate to a location close to the jungle's edge, arriving just before dawn. Lt. Alers-Hankey, Sgt. Burrell and the inspector moved forward in

The MRLA had, meanwhile, been seriously whittled down. By mid-1958, after daring stratagems by SEPs and Special Branch officers had brought about the mass surrenders of 120 CTs in Perak and 160 in Johore, little more than 1,000 of the enemy remained at large, most of them in the north. As terrorist incidents and contacts by the Security Forces reduced to 12 and 27 respectively in 1959, more and more areas were declared 'White' until, on 31 July 1960, restrictions ended everywhere except in zones of Perlis, Kedah and Kelantan along the Thailand border. On the other side of this border the last 500 hard-core terrorists of the MRLA had taken sanctuary with the MCP's Secretary-General, Chin Peng: and there, apparently, the ageing survivors are still holed up to this day, living as dacoits in the almost impenetrable jungle. The Malayan Emergency was now officially declared ended.

Police Aboriginal Guards, armed with single-barrelled shotgun, at Fort Kemar, Upper Perak, 1956–57. The PAGs wore uniforms of a sort but many preferred to remain barefoot, as shown. (Imperial War Museum)

Available figures indicate that the following numbers of Security Forces personnel lost their lives during the conflict: British Army 340, RM Commandos 30, RAF 76, Gurkha Rifles 169, Australian Army 15, RAAF 12, New Zealand Army 10, NZAF 5, Malayan Army 128, Malayan Police 1,347, plus small numbers of African, Fijian and Sarawak personnel. Known Communist losses were: 6,707 killed, 1,296 captured and 2,681 surrendered. There were also 2,473 civilian fatalities and 810 missing.

More than 100,000 British soldiers served in the Malayan campaign. The opportunity to write and to illustrate their story, and that of their Gurkha, Malayan and other Commonwealth allies, has been a great privilege, for which the author and the artist—both infantry veterans of the campaign—are deeply grateful.

The Plates

Jungle Uniforms

Olive Greens (OGs) were manufactured in India; they were recognisable by the unpleated bush shirt pockets with 'square' flaps, and by the map and field-dressing pockets with metal buttons on the front of the slacks. The 1950 pattern Jungle Greens (JGs) were made in the UK; these had pleated shirt pockets, and a side-mounted map pocket on the slacks. These two 'Aertex' uniforms were the most numerous on issue. A third pattern, preceding the 1950 JGs, was made from very dark green drill, and had slacks which were similar to the OG design but with four waist-belt loops. There was another pattern of shirt which had patches on the shoulders and rubber buttons which perished with use.

A1: Captain, Australian Infantry; Kota Tinggi, Johore, 1953
This instructor at the FARELF (Far East Land Forces) Training Centre wears the familiar Australian bush hat and pale-green jungle uniform of Second World War vintage. He holds a .45in. ACP de Lisle silent carbine designed to 'take out' sentries without alerting other terrorists in a camp. The artist recalls his own instruction in its

use: 'The Aussie instructor fired the carbine into a bamboo-brake. The weapon gave a slight "Huff!" but the bullet, travelling with almost unbelievable slowness through the bamboo, made a noise like a boy running down railings with a stick . . . and there was no guarantee, of course, that the sentry would obligingly die instantly and noiselessly.'

A2: Company Sergeant Major, 1st Bn., The Royal Hampshire Regiment; Bentong, Pahang, 1954
Dressed as for a regimental duty, this CSM wears his rank crown on a leather strap on his right wrist. The formation sign of the 18th Independent Infantry Brigade—crossed white bayonet and *kukri* on a red background—can be seen on the sleeve of the 1950 pattern JG bush shirt. The slip-on shoulder titles were unique to this regiment and worn by Other Ranks only. The bands of colour varied with each company—A being green, B yellow, HQ white, etc. The US Presidential Unit Citation, above the formation sign, indicates an ex-Gloster survivor of the epic battle of the Imjin River in Korea. (For administration purposes in the United Kingdom the infantry regiments of the south-western counties were grouped into the 'Wessex Brigade Group'; there was a good deal of cross-posting between battalions, to bring units up to strength as needed.)

Rare night combat photograph of Bren gunner and riflemen of C company, 1st Loyal Regiment, based at Siputeh, during a midnight encounter with a CT gang in the jungle in 1957. (Imperial War Museum)

A3: General Sir Gerald Templer, High Commissioner of Malaya; Kuala Lumpur, 1952
Wearing a tailor-made uniform, Sir Gerald has standard badges of rank supplemented by the cypher of ADC to the Sovereign on his shoulder-strap. His General Officer's badge is worn on the red band of his Service Dress cap. Decoration ribbons on his chest include KBE, DSO, British War Medal 1914–20, Victory Medal, GSM, 1939–45 Star, Africa Star, Italy Star, France and Germany Star, Defence Medal, War Medal 1939–45 with 'Mention' clasp, King George VI Coronation 1937, and five foreign decorations.

A4: Sergeant, Glider Pilot Regiment, early 1950s
As the glider faded from military use in the post-Second World War years, the glider pilots moved to reconnaissance and liaison duties flying various Marks of Auster 'spotter' aircraft. Though supplied and maintained by the RAF, the Austers were under the operational control of the Army and were flown principally by NCO pilots of the Glider Pilot Regiment. Their missions were extremely hazardous, involving many crashes in remote jungle terrain. The sergeant wears the badge of his regiment on the maroon beret of Airborne Forces. His OG bush shirt shows the Army Flying badge above his medal ribbons, while his sleeves display the formation sign of HQ Malaya Command—a yellow *kris* (Malay dagger) on a green background.

A5: Gurkha Rifleman, 1950s
This figure, whose badge—the black metal plumes and scroll of the Prince of Wales, identifying the 2nd King Edward VII's Own Gurkha Rifles—is just visible on a red patch at the left side of his distinctive 'doubled' Gurkha hat, is typical of the soldiers who served in the eight battalions of the Brigade of Gurkhas and support units of the 17th Division. His 1950 JG shirt is impeccably starched and pressed, and displays the General Service Medal (Malaya) and the formation sign of the 17th Gurkha Division—crossed white *kukris* on a dark green background.

A6: Formation sign of 99th Gurkha Brigade
Crossed white *kukris* on a red background.

Men of 22 SAS move out to their aircraft for Operation 'Termite', 8 July 1954—the largest parachute operation carried out by the regiment during the Malayan campaign. See Plate G1 for detail of 1954 Abseil Equipment worn by these troopers. (21 SAS)

A7: Formation sign of 2nd Guards Brigade
Crossed white *kukri* and bayonet on a background of blue, red and blue horizontal bands. By July 1950, both the 3rd Bn., Grenadier Guards and 2nd Bn., Coldstream Guards had departed, leaving only the 2nd Bn., Scots Guards. The *kukri*-and-bayonet motif was retained, on a red background, by the then redesignated 18th Independent Infantry Brigade.

B1: Constable, Federation of Malaya Police, 1949–50
Wearing a dark blue velvet *songkok* (Malay hat), locally manufactured khaki drill (KD) short-sleeved shirt and shorts, dark blue hose and white anklets, this constable carries the magazines for his Mark V Sten gun in a 1937 pattern ammunition pouch clipped to his white webbing belt. Their casualties prove that the Police were very much first in the line of fire.

B2: Woman Police Constable, early 1950s
Women PCs, including Specials, were particularly required for searches of female rubber tappers during food control checks, or of detained female terrorist suspects. This girl wears a dark blue beret and KD pleated uniform-dress. Like the previous figure, she displays a dark blue lanyard running from the left shoulder to a whistle in the breast pocket.

B3: Commissioner of Police Arthur E. Young, 1952
Early in 1952 Commissioner Young was seconded from the City of London to replace Col. Gray as Police Commissioner of Malaya. Young helped the force to gain public goodwill by stressing the goal of community service. Accordingly he introduced a new police badge which included two clasped hands and the motto 'Bersedia Berkhidmat' (Ready to Serve). He is here wearing a silver-laced dark blue peaked cap, police lanyard, KD short-sleeved bush shirt worn in jacket form, shorts, and KD hose with dark blue tops. His dark blue shoulder boards show the silver rank insignia of Commissioner of Police—a crossed dagger and sheath in a wreath, under a crown.

B4: Police Aboriginal Guard; Fort Kemar, Upper Perak, 1955
There were 19 Sections of PAGs in 1955. As aborigines gained confidence in the Security Forces many former members of the Communist Asal Protection Corps changed sides and joined the AAPs or PAGs. Dressed in KD shirt and shorts, the PAG wears sheaves of menkuang grass

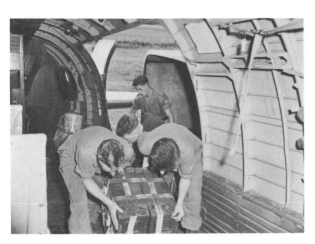

Men of 55 Company, RASC loading 3in. mortar bombs into a Valetta at Kuala Lumpur for parachuting to the 3rd Malay regiment on operations, 1957. The heroic 55 Company lost 43 dead in air crashes through their determination to ensure that patrols in the jungle received their rations and other supplies, no matter how bad the weather conditions. (Imperial War Museum)

stuck through his head-band, and is armed with a single-barrelled shotgun.

B5: Silver metal badge of the Federation of Malaya Police
As worn on the head-dresses of three figures on this page.

C1: Junior NCO, 1st Bn., The Royal Hampshire Regiment, 1954
The yellow triangular symbol of A Company at both front and rear of this NCO's jungle hat, and the red recognition band (colours were changed for each operation) were designed to prevent troops from shooting each other. Dressed in a 'faded to brown' OG shirt, and JG slacks which are tied outside his canvas and rubber jungle boots to deter leeches, he carries a .30cal. M2 carbine and 50 rounds of ammunition—two 'banana clips' loaded with 20 rounds each and one 15-round magazine containing ten. His waist belt of salvaged airdrop lashing supports a 1944 pattern water bottle and holder, a native *parang* knife and a locally-made SMG magazine pouch. His 1937 pattern pack has '44 pattern shoulder straps with specially made sponge rubber pads; it contains a four-day supply of tinned 'compo' rations, a hexamine cooker, hammock, poncho-cape, change of clothes and other personal kit. A second canteen is suspended from the pack containing a quart of

rum. The NCO's map is enclosed in a flat 50-cigarette tin, which fits nicely into the map pocket of his slacks. Round his neck is a lanyard which leads to a prismatic compass in his breast pocket, and a cord to which is attached a vital jungle item —a tin opener. The limp cloth jungle hat was often stiffened into some preferred shape by ingenious use of wire and stitching—sometimes achieving heights of individuality which attracted the wrath of higher authority!

By 1953–54 there were enough of the American semi-automatic carbines available to be more widely distributed—previously there were only two per platoon. They were naturally quicker-firing than the bolt-action British rifles, had less kick, and suffered fewer misfires through ammunition deterioration in the humid climate.

C2: Private, 1st Bn., The Devonshire Regiment, June 1948
Clad in khaki beret, OG uniform, ammunition boots and anklets and 1937 pattern equipment, this figure is typical of the troops rushed to guard key points when the Emergency was first declared. He is armed with a .303 Bren LMG Mark III. Jungle boots and short No. 5 rifles were issued to the troops within two months of the insurrection, but 1944 pattern equipment was not generally allocated until early 1950.

C3: Guardsman, 2nd Bn., The Scots Guards, 1949
Similarly dressed and equipped to the previous figure apart from his 'cheesecutter' SD cap, the guardsman holds an 'EY' rifle—an SMLE No. 1 fitted with a discharger cup to project No. 36 grenades with seven-second fuses to a maximum range of just over 200 yards. It could also fire No. 80 (white phosphorus) grenades. The EY had one great advantage over the infantry squad's 2in. mortar—its time fuse. The mortar bomb was armed to explode on impact from shortly after leaving the barrel, and almost invariably did so when it struck the jungle canopy, either on the way up or the way down.

D1: Infantry signaller, 1951
The 31lb. Wireless Set No. 68, plus satchel containing headphones, microphone and box of spare valves, 90ft. of coiled wire aerial, the signaller's

34

personal kit wrapped in his poncho-cape and roped to the top of his set, with the added weight of his No. 5 rifle and 50 rounds of ammunition, all made a formidable load to carry on a jungle trek. The figure depicted wears his 1944 pattern ammunition pouches on his hips rather than in the regulation and constricting position on the front of the waist-belt. In this scenario the signaller is using the muzzle of his rifle and his left hand to convey the sign for 'enemy camp ahead'—the inverted V of a roof.

D2: Infantry leading scout, early 1950s
Meanwhile the scout, observing the terrorist camp, slips the safety slide off his Owen SMG. His rations and personal kit are carried both in his 1944 pattern pack and in the rolled poncho-cape strapped beneath it. Note rubber-and-canvas 'plimsolls' attached to the pack. A scout needed a lot of nerve, and had to be constantly alert for signs of human passage or of the enemy lurking in ambush.

D3: Iban tracker, early 1950s
Having followed a trail provided either by footprints or chopped or broken foliage, the Iban crouches down while the patrol moves up to attack. Most Ibans had long hair gathered in a loose bun at the nape of the neck, pierced and stretched ear-lobes, gold teeth, and tattoos in tribal designs covering many parts of their bodies. This Iban displays his *parang* with a lock of human hair dangling from the hilt, taken—he would no doubt claim—from a head lopped off during the 'old' head-hunting days in Sarawak. Though some Ibans were excellent trackers, others were markedly less adept at junglecraft than their reputation suggested.

E1: Company commander, MRLA, early 1950s
The uniforms worn by CTs were made from readily available KD cloth that was extensively used in the Federation. Stolen JG or OG uniforms were also sometimes worn. MCP State, District or Branch Committee Members were appointed as officers or political commissars to MRLA fighting units. This commander wears the standard pattern of CT cap with five peaks formed by the seams, a cloth chinstrap and covered buttons. In February 1949 it was recommended that the normal single embroidered red star on the cap be replaced by three stars to represent the three Malayan races theoretically involved. This was not, however, universally adopted. The pistol (normally only issued to officers) is a Police Smith and Wesson .38in. complete with leather holster and ammunition pouch. The artist recalls: 'Terrorist weapons, unless recently taken from the Security Forces, were usually in very poor condition. There were few armourers or tools and no firing ranges. Weapons, and especially ammunition, deteriorated rapidly in the jungle. A captured Thompson SMG (as illustrated) particularly comes to mind—worn, rusty, crudely repaired and with the woodwork in a state of virtual disintegration—I doubt very much that it would have functioned.'

E2: Female member of the Min Yuen, 1950s
Many women were involved in Min Yuen (People's Movement) organising food supplies, funds, clothing and other requirements for the jungle units. This Chinese girl wears typical light khaki blouse and black trousers. She holds a locally-manufactured Communist flag, proclaiming the message: 'Through violence we shall

1957: L/Cpl. Hughes, 22 SAS, kitted up for patrol with a substantially packed Bergen rucksack and armed with a sawn-off Browning automatic shotgun. (Imperial War Museum)

Sgt. Stubbs, 1st King's Dragoon Guards, commanding a Ferret armoured car covering the Mantin Pass between Kuala Lumpur and Seremban while on VIP escort duty, 1957. (Imperial War Museum)

conquer!' Ten per cent of the personnel of MRLA fighting units were also women and wore KD or JG uniforms like the men, though they normally filled non-combatant roles.

E3: Soldier, 32nd Independent Platoon, MRLA; Mentekab, Pahang, 1954

In 1954 the 32nd Independent Platoon was mainly composed of Indians and about 50 strong. The CT depicted wears standard KD cap and uniform, the slacks being Federation of Malaya Police pattern. Japanese-type cotton puttees are wound round his legs above canvas-and-rubber basket-ball boots. Equipment includes a 1937 British 'big pack' with a plastic 'table-cloth' shelter-half under the flap, Japanese water-bottle, *parang* jungle knife, and a five-pocket drill cloth and tape cartridge belt with toggle fastenings. His rifle is an old SMLE Mark III. The sheets of gaily patterned plastic from civilian sources were widely used as waterproofs by the MRLA.

F1: Police Sergeant; Jungle Squad HQ, Sungei Bakap, Province Wellesley, 1951

The author had the privilege of accompanying this Sikh sergeant on an operation in April 1951. Up to that date the sergeant had personally killed five bandits with his five-shot, Belgian-manu-factured Browning automatic 12-gauge shotgun. He is clad in a KD turban and police pattern JGs, which were a bluer green than the Army issue and had a map pocket on each thigh. He also carries an SMLE sword-bayonet attached to his cartridge-belt.

F2: Police Superintendent, Kuala Lumpur, 1948

'Two-Gun' Bill Stafford, Officer-in-Charge of Detectives, KL, was the man responsible for killing the high-ranking terrorist Lau Yew (see main text). He is shown here wearing a bush hat, KD shirt, JG slacks and hockey boots. Apart from his M1 carbine he is also armed with a Smith and Wesson .38 Police Special revolver in a shoulder-holster; suspended from his belt is an Army issue machete.

F3: Aborigine woman, mid-1950s

The aborigines of the Temiar, Semai and other tribes of the central mountain range were alternately wooed and armed by both sides. This Temiar girl is clad in a colourful cloth sarong, and clutches her single-barrelled shotgun with evident satisfaction.

F4: Aborigine, mid-1950s

Wearing a bark loin-cloth and head-band, this male aborigine prepares to shoot his 8ft. bamboo blowpipe, which was normally accurate up to 35 feet. The eight-inch darts were tipped with a paralytic poison manufactured from a boiled mixture of the saps of the Ipoh tree and Ipoh creeper. According to its strength this poison could bring death within a few minutes after entering the bloodstream, or might take as long as an hour.

F5: Sergeant, Gurkha Rifles, 1948

The unmistakable Gurkha hat and *kukri* identify this figure, as do the Rifle-green stripes on his sleeve. He is wearing 1937 pattern equipment and is armed with a Mark V Sten gun, and apart from the features mentioned is dressed and equipped in all respects like his British comrades.

G1: Trooper, 22nd Special Air Service Regiment, 1954
Shown wearing the familiar maroon Airborne beret worn by SAS until 1957, to be replaced when he emplanes by the paratrooper's helmet at his feet, this trooper is clad in OG uniform with his pack slung upon his chest beneath his early-pattern, sleeveless jump smock. Several pairs of puttees are wound round his calves and ankles to provide support when he parachutes into the jungle canopy. He carries a felt valise containing a 240ft. roll of 1 in. webbing, which he will attach to a branch in the tree-tops, and then lower himself to the ground, the webbing running through D-rings on his 'bikini' harness. This method of descent, known as 'abseiling', nearly always involved some injuries, and there were occasional fatalities. The trooper is wearing an X-type parachute and no reserve. Also seen is the butt of his M1 carbine, while strapped to his right leg is a Fairbairn-Sykes fighting knife.

G2: Royal Marine Commando, Perak, 1951
The 3rd RM Commando Brigade arrived in Malaya during May to June 1950 and soon established a tough reputation in the jungles of Perak. Dressed for vehicle escort or guard duty at his Troop's permanent base, this Marine wears a green Commando beret, OG shirt, pre-1950 pattern slacks and jungle boots. The belt is 1944 pattern and the canvas magazine pouch is locally made. His weapon is the excellent Australian Mark II Owen gun, which was heavier, more stable and more reliable than the Sten.

G3: Corporal, 1st Bn., The King's Own Yorkshire Light Infantry; Penang, Minden Day, 1950
Five of the six British infantry regiments which fought at the battle of Minden in 1759 commemorate the victory on 1 August every year by wearing roses above their cap badges. The

Gunners of A Troop, 75th Battery, 148th Field Regiment RA run to man their 25pdr. field guns for action against CTs in the Tampin area of Negri Sembilan, 1957. (Imperial War Museum)

L/Cpl. Sage, 1st South Wales Borderers, adjusts a tracker dog's harness before setting out in search of the enemy near Tampoi, 1957. (Imperial War Museum)

KOYLI corporal shown here wears starched JG shirt and shorts, rifle-green beret and hose and light green puttees. His sleeve displays the formation sign of 17th Gurkha Division, above his distinctive Light Infantry green chevrons on white backing.

G4: Captain, 1st Bn., The Cameronians (Scottish Rifles); Segamat, Johore, 1952

This officer is clad in starched, tailor-made JGs with black metal regimental buttons and rank stars. He also wears a Rifle-green glengarry with a black edge, tourie and tails; a black lanyard, and a black webbing belt. His hose are Rifle-green flecked with white and the tops have crossed white stripes and lighter green diamonds with dark blue stripes; the garter flashes are also green. Unlike the previous figure, his puttees are a light shade of khaki and are wound to finish on the inside of the leg. His upper sleeve shows the formation sign of a golden cockerel on a black ground, appropriate to 40 Division in Hong Kong, whence the Cameronians had departed for Malaya in April 1950.

G5: Squadron Leader, 81 Squadron RAF; Tengah, Singapore, 1959

Climbing into his Meteor PR10 jet fighter, this pilot is wearing jungle boots as part of his survival gear in case of the necessity for ejection over the jungle. He wears a pale blue-grey Mark IV flying suit and a chrome-yellow life preserver. His protective helmet is a silver Mark 1A Bone Dome with a polaroid visor and a type G cellular cotton inner helmet. His oxygen mask would be RAF issue type P or Q with chain-tensioned face plates to facilitate pressure breathing up to 56,000 feet. The background shows an airman of RAF maintenance staff stripped for work upon a Valetta transport aircraft.

H1: Captain, 2nd Bn., The King's African Rifles, 1953

The 2nd KARs arrived in Malaya in July 1953. Capt. H. R. Gilliver—known by the artist during a later three-month attachment to 1st Royal Hampshires—here displays undyed guinea fowl feathers above the 2nd KARs' badge on his bush hat; black metal rank stars, shoulder titles and regimental buttons, and a black officer's lanyard.

H2: Private, 1st Bn., The Gordon Highlanders, 1952

Wearing the familiar khaki Balmoral of Scottish infantry regiments, the soldier wears an OG shirt displaying regimental shoulder titles, the GSM ribbon, and the formation sign of 17th Gurkha Division. Ammunition for his No. 5 rifle is carried in a cloth bandolier worn apron-fashion below the tartan stable belt of the Gordons. His arms show the results of visits to one of Malaya's many tattoo parlours.

H3: Lieutenant, 848 Naval Air Squadron, 1953
This pilot of one of the squadron's ten Sikorski S-55 Whirlwind helicopters wears a Royal Navy officer's beret and lieutenant's ranking with Army JG uniform. He holds the handset of a Wireless Set No. 62, used for air-ground communications.

H4: Trooper, 11th Hussars, 1953
Taking over from the 13th/18th Hussars, the 11th were responsible for patrolling the roads of South Malaya. This trooper wears audio-frequency headphones for the Wireless Set No. 19 of his armoured car, and privately-purchased goggles over the 11th Hussars' distinctive cherry-and-brown badgeless beret.

H5: Iban tracker, 1952
Wearing the badge of the Suffolk Regiment—to which he is attached for operations—on his dark blue beret, the tracker shows the typical pierced, stretched ear-lobes and tribal tattoos of these small, sturdy men from Sarawak. Among British soldiers the legends (and, probably, myths!) about their bloodthirsty habits were legion.

H6: Private, Malay Regiment, 1955
Seven battalions of the Malay Regiment took part in the campaign. All wore the green *songkok* and regimental badge, as illustrated.

H7: Formation sign, HQ Malaya Command
A yellow *kris* (traditional Malay dagger) on a green background.

H8: Air Despatch organisation (incl. 55 Coy., RASC)
Responsible for supplying troops in the jungle—a yellow Dakota aircraft on a blue background.

Soldiers of 1st New Zealand Regiment, all armed with 7.62mm self-loading rifles, leave an aborigine village while on patrol in Perak, 1958. (New Zealand Defence Department)

Notes sur les planches en couleur

A1 Instructeur en armes à feu avec une carabine 'silencieuse' De Lisle. **A2** Insigne de grade porté sur une bande au poignet; insigne régimental sur les pattes d'épaule avec les rayures vertes de la Compagnie A; insigne de la 18th Brigade sur la manche. **A3** Insignes standard de grade; l'emblème royal sur la patte d'épaule indique un ancien aide-de-camp du roi; casquette de commandant. **A4** Pilote d'avion de reconnaissance; cette unité portait encore le béret rouge des forces aéroportées. **A5** Insigne du régiment—les plumes du Prince de Galles—pour le *2nd Gurkha Rifles*, sur une pièce rapportée rouge cousue sur le côté gauche du chapeau des Gurkhas. Insigne de la *17th Gurkha Division* sur la manche. **A6** *99th Gurkha Brigade*. **A7** *2nd Guards Brigade*.

B1 Chapeau malais bleu foncé, fanion bleu foncé et chaussettes, portées avec un uniforme khaki clair par les unités de police. **B2** Version féminine de l'uniforme précédent. **B3** Uniforme de police pour officier supérieur. **B4** Uniforme incomplet de police auxiliaire. **B5** Insigne de calot de la police.

C1 Insignes de couvre-chefs: le triangle identifie la Compagnie A, la bande rouge étant adoptée par l'unité pour une opération particulière. La carabine M2, un équipement principalement de modèle 1944, des bottes de jungle et des provisions de rhum et d'eau. La carte est rangée dans un étui de métal pour 50 cigarettes. Les couvre-chefs étaient souvent modelés selon les goûts individuels avec du fil de fer ou bien étaient cousus. **C2** Béret khaki porté en temps habituel, avec l'uniforme standard vert-jungle et un équipement de 1937. **C3** Semblable à la tenue précédente, mais avec un chapeau des Gardes. Le fusil a un lance-grenades, plus utile en jungle que les mortiers, dont les projectiles explosent souvent trop près s'ils sont arrêtés par les arbres.

D1 Notez le fardeau excessif de l'opérateur-radio pour une patrouille en jungle. Avec le canon du fusil No 5 et sa main gauche, il mimique un toit: camp ennemi en vue. **D2** L'homme de tête d'une patrouille garde sa mitraillette Owen armée et pointée constamment. **D3** Les Ibans, chasseurs de têtes de Bornéo, portaient un uniforme anglais mais conservaient aussi des caractéristiques tribales comme le *parang*, couteau agrémenté de cheveux.

E1 Calot communiste de forme typique, avec un insigne en trois étoiles représentant les trois races qui théoriquement formaient le mouvement terroriste. **E2** Vêtement typique en khaki clair noir, avec un drapeau: 'Nous vaincrons par le force!' Le mouvement pouvait compter sur la participation active de nombreuses militantes. **E3** Cette unité était composée d'Indiens. Uniforme et équipement typiques; celui-ci est complet, ce qui est inhabituel. Les feuilles de plastique d'origine non-militaire, étaient souvent utilisées en capes ou en tentes imperméables.

F1 Les fusils de chasse étaient des armes habituelle et efficaces dans la jungle. Turban khaki avec insigne et tenue règlementaire de la police, d'un ton plus bleu que celle de l'armée. **F2** 'Two-Gun Bill' Stafford, qui tua le chef communiste Lau Yew. **F3**, **F4**, Les Aborigines utilisaient leurs sarbacanes mais on leur donnait aussi des fusils de chasse quand on les savaient loyaux aux troupes gouvernementales. **F5** Le chapeau, les chevrons verts et le *kukri*, (couteau) sont tout ce qui distingue un Gurkha des troupes anglaises.

G1 Pour être parachuté dans la jungle, il porte plusieurs bandes molletières; il porte son sac sur la poitrine sous sa vareuse de saut et à environ 80 mètres de courroie de toile pour se laisser glisser du haut des arbres jusqu'au sol, ce qui était une technique très dangereuse. Les SAS ont porté le béret rouge des troupes aéroportées jusqu'en 1957. **G2** De garde au campement de son unité, ce Marine ne porte pas d'équipement de campagne; la cartouchière pour le fusil Owen était fabriquée localement. **G3** Tenue d'apparat avec le béret vert foncé et les chevrons de grade du *Light Infantry*. Les régiments qui participèrent à la bataille de Minden en 1759 portent une rose à leur calot le jour commemoratif, en souvenir de la fameuse charge à travers la roseraie de Minden. **G4** Insigne de manche de la *40th Division* de Hong Kong, d'où cette unité fut transférée. Le calot du régiment et autres détails particuliers sont en vert foncé et noir. **G5** Combinaison de vol Mk.IV et casque Mk.IA, plus des bottes de jungle, précaution vitale au cas où il aurait eu à sauter en parachute au-dessus de la jungle.

H1 Insigne du régiment et plumes de pintade au chapeau, avec l'insigne noir de tous les bataillons du *King's African Rifles*. **H2** Insigne de manche de la *17th Gurkha Division*, et motif particulier au régiment, du 'ceinturon d'écurie'. **H3** Pilote d'hélicoptère portant le béret d'officier de la Royal Navy et l'insigne de grade sur une tenue de l'armée. **H4** On ne mettait pas d'insigne sur ce béret bien distinct marron et rouge. **H5** Traqueurs Ibans avec leurs tatouages typiques et les lobes d'oreilles étirés. **H6** Toutes les unités du régiment malais portaient le *songkok*, un chapeau vert foncé. **H7** Quartier-Général, Région militaire de Malaisie. **H8** Unités d'expéditions aériennes.

Farbtafeln

A1 Waffenausbilder mit 'De Lisle' 'schallgedämpftem' Karabiner. **A2** Rangabzeichen am Gelenkriemen; regimentale Abzeichen an den Schulterriemen, mit den grünen Streifen der A Kompanie; Abzeichen der 18. Brigade am Ärmel. **A3** Normale Rangabzeichen; königliches Chiffre am Schulterriemen markiert den einstigen Dienst als 'ADC' zum König; Generals-Offiziersmütze. **A4** Pilot eines Aufklärungsflugzeuges; diese Einheit trug noch das rote Beret der Luftlandetruppen. **A5** Regimentsabzeichen—Federbüschel des Prinzen von Wales, für die '2nd Gurkha Rifles'—auf einem roten Flecken auf der linken Seite des Gurkha Hutes. Das Abzeichen der '17th Gurkha Div.' am Ärmel. **A6** 99th Gurkha Brigade. **A7** 2nd Guards Brigade.

B1 Dunkelblauer malaiischer Hut, dunkelblauer Faljereep und Socken mit heller khakifarbener Uniform von den Polizeieinheiten getragen. **B2** Die Frauenversion der vorausgegangenen Uniform. **B3** Höhere Offiziersversion der Polizeiuniform. **B4** Teiluniform eines Hilfspolizisten. **B5** Polizei-Mützenabzeichen.

C1 Hutabzeichen: Dreieck lässt die A Kompanie erkennen, das rote Band wurde von der ganzen Einheit für eine spezifische Operation angenommen. M2 Karabiner, meistens Ausrüstung nach dem 1944er Muster, Dschungelstiefel, Wasser- und Rumbehälter; Karte, in einer 50er Zigarettenbüchse aufbewahrt. Die Hüte wurden oft mit Draht und Faden zu bevorzugten Formen versteift. **C2** Khakifarbenes Beret, getragen, wenn nicht im 'Busch', mit dschungelgrüner Grunduniform und 1937er Ausrüstung. **C3** Dieselbe Ausstattung wie vorhergehend, jedoch Gardehut. Gewehr mit Granatenwerferzusatz, nützlicher als Möser im Dschungel, wo die Mörserbomben oft zu früh explodierten, wenn sie Bäume getroffen haben.

D1 Bemerke die erschöpfende Last für eine Dschungelpatrouille, die von einem Funker getragen wird. Mit der Mündung des Nr. 5 Gewehres und der linken Hand macht er ein stilles Zeichen eines 'Daches'—'Feindliches Lager vorne'. **D2** Das führende Mitglied einer Patrouille hält seine Owen Maschinenpistole zu jeder Zeit entsichert und in Schussbereitschaft. **D3** Iban Stammesmänner, Kopfjäger von Borneo, trugen britische Uniformen, behielten jedoch Stammeseigenarten, wie das 'parang' Messer, verziert mit Menschenhaar.

E1 Kommunistische Mütze von typischer Form mit dem Dreisternenabzeichen, welches drei Rassen andeutet, die—der Theorie nachdie Terroristenbewegung ins Leben gerufen haben. **E2** Typische hellkhakifarbene und schwarze Kleidung mit Flagge: 'Durch Gewalt werden wir erobern!' Viele Frauen spielten eine aktive Rolle in der Bewegung. **E3** Diese Einheit bestand aus Inder. Typische, jedoch ungewöhnlich komplette, Uniform und Ausrüstung. Zivile Plastikplanen wurden oft als wasserfeste Umhänge und Zelte benutzt.

F1 Die Schrotflinte war eine übliche und wirksame Dschungelwaffe. Khakifarbener Turban mit Abzeichen; und für die Polizei ausgegebene grüne Uniform, von blauerer Schattierung als der Armeetyp. **F2** 'Zwei-Kanonen-Bill' Stafford, der den Kommunistenführer Lau Yew tötete. **F3**, **F4** Die Ureinwohner benutzten die traditionellen Blaspfeifen, erhielten jedoch auch Schrotflinten, wenn sie sich den Regierungstruppen gegenüber als vertrauenswürdig erwiesen. **F5** Hut, grüne Winkel und das 'Kuhri' Messer sind das, was diesen Gurkha von den britischen Truppen unterscheidet.

G1 Für den Fallschirmabsprung in den Dschungel trägt er verschiedene Lagen von Beinbandagen; sein Pack wird auf der Brust unter dem Sprunganzug getragen; und er trägt 250 Fuss Leinengürtelzeug mit sich, womit er sich von Baumspitzen zum Boden herablassen kann. Diese Methode war sehr gefährlich. Die SAS trug bis zum Jahr 1957 rote Luftlandeberets. **G2** Bei der Wache im Lager seiner Einheit trägt dieser 'Marineinfanterist' keine Feldausrüstung; der Munitionsbeutel für das Owen Gewehr wurde örtlich hergestellt. **G3** Paradeuniform mit dunkelgrünem Beret und Rangabzeichen der 'Light Infantry'. Am Jahrestag der Schlacht von Minden, 1759, tragen die Regimenter, die dort kämpften, eine Rose an ihren Mützen um dem berühmten Angriff durch den Rosengarten bei Minden zu gedenken. **G4** Ärmelabzeichen der 40.Div. in Hong Kong, von wo diese Einheit verlegt wurde. Regimentale Beret und andere Eigenarten in dunkelgrün und schwarz. **G5** Mk.IV Fliegeranzug; Mk.IA Helm; sowie Dschungelstiefel als Teil einer Überlebensausrüstung im Falle, dass er in den Dschungel abspringen muss.

H1 Regimentales Abzeichen und Perlhuhnfedern am Hut; sowie schwarze Abzeichen aller Bataillons der 'King's African Rifles'. **H2** 17. Gurkha Div. Ärmelabzeichen; sowie besonderes regimentales Muster des 'Stallgürtels'. **H3** Hubschrauberpilot mit dem Beret eines Offiziers der königlichen Marine und Rangabzeichen an Armeekleidung. **H4** Kein Abzeichen wurde an dem besonderen regimentalen braunroten Beret getragen. **H5** Typische Tätowierung und Ohrendehnung der Iban Spurhalter. **H6** Alle Einheiten des malaischen Regiments trugen den 'songkok' Hut in dunkelgrün, Malaisches Kommando. **H7** Hauptquartier, Malaisches Kommando. **H8** Luftversorgungseinheiten.